3/31/99

Dear Kevin,

Happy 12th

Love,
Grandma D

Searching for Heroes

THE QUEST OF A YANKEE BATBOY

JOE CARRIERI

Carrieri, Joe
    Searching for heroes, the quest of a Yankee batboy / Joe Carrieri
        p.   cm.
    ISBN 0-9644701-0-1

Carlyn Publications, Inc.
c/o Carrieri & Carrieri

200 Old Country Road
Mineola, New York 11501
1-516-248-1188

Printed in the United States of America

This book is dedicated to my wife, Marilyn,
our children, Lynn, Joey, Chris, Mike, Steve, and Jessica,
and grandchildren, Marilyn, Lauren, Matt, and D.J.

Acknowledgment

I cannot possibly acknowledge all the people who played a part in the formation of my life and who thereby contributed to the creation of this book. There are so many friends, teachers, colleagues, associates, and partners. Suffice it to say that I will be ever grateful to my parents, who instilled in me the values I possess, and who encouraged me as batboy and lawyer. Thanks to my big brother, Ralph J. Carrieri, for getting me the job of Yankee batboy and for his guidance, both in my old South Bronx neighborhood and, later, at Yankee Stadium. Thanks to my law partner and nephew, Ralph R. Carrieri, for his encouragement; to Brother Colombo for letting me skip school to attend to my duties at Yankee Stadium and for his insight; to Pete Sheehy, the Yankees' clubhouse man, for guiding me through the hierarchy of visiting batboy, ballboy and batboy; to all the Yankee players, especially Phil Rizzuto, who watched over me as a young boy travelling from city to city on the summer road trips with the team. Thanks to Joe DiMaggio for his inspiration. I was privileged to have known him and all the Yankees from the era 1949-1955. Thanks to Michael Tobin for his creative and technical help in designing the book and preparing it to go to press; to Don McIntosh for his assistance in reproducing the photographs appearing herein; to William J. Connolly for his photographic memory for details and for help in proofreading; to Don Wilkens and Jack Flynn who read the early drafts and provided input; to Helen McNamara and Angela Malizia for typing early drafts; and to Judge Lindley Miller and Barbara Miller for their support.

Finally, my very special thanks and appreciation to Gerald A. Tobin, collaborator and editor on this endeavor, whose hard work, dedication, and persistence helped make *Searching for Heroes* a reality. The fast pace of *Searching for Heroes* is a tribute to the style and clarity of Mr. Tobin's writing.

Foreword

From 1949 to 1955 I was the batboy for the New York Yankees. For me, a kid from the South Bronx of New York City, it was the experience of a lifetime to be in Yankee Stadium with my boyhood heroes.

It was also an extraordinary time to be wearing the Yankee pinstripes. I was there when the Yankees won five consecutive World Series (1949-1953); when Casey Stengel, the Ol' Professor, stole the hearts of New York's baseball fans; when, with sadness, Joe DiMaggio finished his extraordinary career; and when up-and-coming Yankee stars like Mickey Mantle, Billy Martin, and Whitey Ford arrived to carry the great Yankee tradition into the next generation.

My seven years with the Yankees were also the formative years of my life. I was a thirteen-year-old seventh-grader when I started and a sophomore at Fordham University when I turned in my uniform.

I almost missed out on this opportunity. To be the batboy, I would have to leave school early for the home games. My principal at St. Jerome's Grammar School, Brother Colombo, bent the rules. He told me I could take the job if I used my time with the Yankees to learn the meaning of greatness through my experiences with baseball's most successful players. And, he told me to write about my experiences.

I took Brother Colombo's admonition seriously. I spent my seven years with the Yankees trying to understand and define the meaning of greatness as I saw it reflected in the lives and experiences of baseball's best players, coaches, and managers. As I grew up, I tried to incorporate what I learned into my own life. That's the theme of *Searching for Heroes*. Although to some, baseball is just a game, to those who love it, baseball will always be a measure of much greater importance, because in the lives of our heroes, we find the best of ourselves, and gather a glimpse of who we are and what we might be if we only take time to learn.

I've also tried to capture the color, flavor, and feel of a simpler time and place. I'd like the reader to taste the sweetness of a Coke after a World Series victory and savor the smell of the infield grass on opening day. I'd also like to introduce many of the important people in my young life. Some of them have familiar names, like DiMaggio, Rizzuto, Stengel, and Robinson. Others, though not nearly as famous, include my mother and father, my brother Ralph, Pete Sheehy the Yankees' clubhouse man, and Charlie DiGiovanna the Dodgers' batboy, a wonderful guy whom most older devoted Dodgers fans well remember.

Today, I'm fifty-something, married with six wonderful children, and a law practice in New York devoted primarily to protecting the rights of children. As I reflect on the goodness of my own life, I recognize a lasting debt to those New York Yankees of forty-some years ago, to my old principal, Brother Colombo, and to so many others.

Searching for Heroes is an expression of my gratitude to the heroes of my young life. It is also an affirmation of the underlying values that supported those who would be role models to a younger generation and an assertion that the age of heroes is not past. Indeed, I believe that a heroism rooted in self-sacrifice, virtue, and excellence is yearning "to be." I hope that my story, as told in following pages, will hasten its rebirth.

The child is father to the man

In December 1987, I received a telephone call from Zeyda Fernandez, a social worker and Director of the Queens Office of St. Christopher-Ottilie, one of the largest private foster care agencies in New York State. For many years, I had been legal counsel to the agency, which has proved a safe harbor for thousands of New York children, including many victims of child abuse. Zeyda was calling about a nine-year-old boy from Queens who had been placed in the care of St. Christopher's by the New York Department of Social Welfare. The boy, Terrence, had been abused by his father, who strapped him to the ceiling pipes in the basement of the family home and then whipped him repeatedly with a belt across his back and shoulders. While Terrence was being beaten, his father forced Terrence's mother and sisters to taunt him for disobeying the father.

Zeyda thought she had seen just about everything during her twenty years in the child welfare system, but she told me that she broke into tears at the sight of the welts on Terrence's back, where the lash marks took the form of a grotesque venetian blind.

Although hardly typical, this should've been a routine case for St. Christopher's. Pending a court hearing, Terrence would be placed by the agency in the protective custody of a temporary guardian for an indefinite period while his father was prosecuted in the criminal justice system. But there was a hitch. Because his father was a diplomat assigned to the United Nations from Zimbabwe, Terrence's father and every member of his immediate family were protected by diplomatic immunity. No American court had the jurisdiction to prosecute Terrence's father or to retain custody of Terrence. Although the child had already been placed with St. Christopher's, the U.S. State Department sought to return him immediately to his family.

Since the first rule in any case of child abuse is to place the victim in a safe environment, the State Department's position seemed incredible. Terrence had already made a favorable adjustment in the home of his foster parents, and the idea of simply handing him over to his tormentor ran counter to the instincts of everyone with any experience in this area. The legal and professional staff at St. Christopher's, as well as the New York Legal Aid Society, decided that this child was worth fighting for. In the midst of a bustling, pressure-filled holiday season, we mobilized in Terrence's defense. In less than a month, we had taken Terrence's case to New York's Family Court, to the Appellate Division of New York's Supreme Court, and, finally, to the Court of Appeals – the State's highest court. But all attempts to convince the courts to hear Terrence's case failed. They simply had no jurisdiction over the matter.

By New Year's Day, it seemed as if the inevitable would occur. Terrence's father had already been deported to Zimbabwe and, it seemed, Terrence would soon be forced to rejoin him and his other family members there.

Although the Family Court ordered the agency to hand over Terrence to the State Department, which would facilitate his return to Zimbabwe, the order was stayed each time an appeal was made. We used the appellate process to play for time. Since we had exhausted all appeals within the New York court system, we attempted to move Terrence's case to the federal courts, hoping that, if all else failed, he might remain in the U.S. under a grant of political asylum.

On New Year's Day, I was called away from my family by representatives of the U.S. State Department. They had an order demanding that St. Christopher's hand over Terrence to them immediately. While I disagreed with the court order, I had no choice but to obey it. I called Terrence's foster father and told him to bring Terrence to my office. When I arrived at my office in Jericho, Long Island, I was greeted by two humorless State Department bureaucrats, court order in hand.

We weren't there long when I received a call from the foster father. He told me he was only a block from my office when Terrence unfastened his seat belt, opened the car door, and tried to jump from the moving vehicle. In the interest of the child's safety, he returned to his home. Shortly after his return, though, Terrence again tried to escape, this time attempting a leap from the second story window of his temporary home.

I explained to the State Department officials that we were dealing with a terrified child, living in fear of his life. But the holiday spirit had passed these two by. They were livid. Back and forth they traveled to the parking lot to talk with their superiors on the car phone. Each time they returned, they issued a new threat. Didn't I know who I was dealing with, they asked me. Didn't I know that I would be held in contempt for disobeying a court order. I was outraged at their suggestion that we have Terrence drugged so that he could be handed over without any fuss. These officials were unwilling or unable to appreciate that Terrence was pleading for his life.

I felt that this was one of those times when rules must be bent if not broken. I dragged my feet, hoping that the federal court would allow us to hold Terrence a bit longer. After a stand-off that lasted hours, my phone rang again. Judge Weinstein of the federal district court had granted a temporary stay pending a hearing on Terrence's petition for political asylum.

We were still alive. An attorney from the Legal Aid Society, which represented Terrence on behalf of the Department of Child Welfare, said that Judge Weinstein would hold the hear-ing at his home the next day, Saturday January 2, 1988.

Based on his ongoing psychological examination of Terrence, Dr. Leonard Gries, the resident psychologist at St. Christopher's, was convinced that Terrence should eventually be reunited with his mother and sisters. But Dr. Gries strongly felt that to return him to Zimbabwe at this point was the worst thing that could happen to him – threatening both his physical and men-tal well-being.

Although we didn't think that Terrence should be separated indefinitely from his family, the petition for political asylum helped us do what was necessary – protect Terrence from immi-nent danger by delaying his return to Zimbabwe.

Dr. Gries, Bob McMahon – the head of St. Christopher's, Tom Ring director of foster care at the agency, and I drove to Judge Weinstein's home in Long Island the next day. Terrence's Legal Aid attorney, Henry Weintraub, also appeared as did Igou Allbray, a Deputy U.S. Attorney representing the State Department.

Given the extraordinary circumstances of the case, Judge Weinstein was willing to hold the hearing in his own dining room during the long holiday weekend. He was obviously sympathetic to Terrence's plight. But, as expected, after hearing our arguments as well as the testimony of Dr. Gries, he ruled that he had no jurisdiction over the matter. He lifted the stay. But Judge Weinstein opened a door for us – just a crack. He ordered that the government had the burden of obtaining custody of Terrence. It was no longer up to St. Christopher's to facilitate Terrence's transfer. The State Department would have to return to court to obtain a writ of habeas corpus meaning that they needed to make an additional court appearance to obtain custody.

This delay allowed us to hold on to Terrence for another day while we appealed Judge Weinstein's order. Custody of the child was the critical issue. Once he was handed over to the State Department, he would be whisked out of the country. If that happened, we would never be able to bring him back to an American court, and we'd never have another opportunity to offer him our protection.

During the hearing at his home, Judge Weinstein had been so impressed by McMahon's interest and concern for Terrence that he appointed him to be Terrence's temporary guardian. McMahon would be Terrence's surrogate parent, looking out for his best interests while he remained in the United States. Terrence could not have received a more able, committed, or savvy protector. In no time, McMahon was on the phone speaking to Senator Moynihan of New York, Congressmen from around the country, and the media. We were making news. The plight of "Terrence of Zimbabwe" was drawing the attention of politicians and the public. His case was editorialized in the Wall Street Journal, became the subject of Congressional hearings, and was even a topic at one of President Reagan's cabinet meetings.

We pressed ahead for a hearing on Terrence's request for political asylum and were petitioning the court to overturn Judge Weinstein's order. The order was stayed pending the appeal and, again, we had a little breathing room. The hearing was set for January 7, 1988 at the Second Circuit Court of Appeals in Manhattan. If we lost at this juncture, the next step was an appeal to the U.S. Supreme Court.

McMahon asked me to be his legal representative in his capacity as Terrence's guardian. Because I would be representing McMahon, I would have an opportunity to present an argument to the three-judge panel that would hear the appeal.

Until this point, the Legal Aid Society had done yeoman's work, spending hundreds of hours researching and developing legal arguments that it hoped would convince the court to grant Terrence's petition for asylum. In court after court, the arguments had failed. By now, there was nothing I could add to the legal arguments that had been so skillfully presented by these attorneys. It was obvious that the court had very little room to maneuver, even if it wanted to.

But I had to do something that would dramatize that failing to protect Terrence would be a crime against our common humanity. I had to do something that hadn't been done before.

On January 7th, the court was packed with spectators and television, newspaper, and radio reporters and commentators. Thanks largely to McMahon, in a matter of days Terrence of Zimbabwe had become an international story, attracting news coverage from every corner of the globe.

I barely heard the legal arguments that were being offered by Mr. Allbray on behalf of the State Department and those offered by the Legal Aid Society for Terrence. By now, I knew them by heart.

I lost myself in the court's bright lights and the blur of the crowded room, remembering a day so many years before when a little boy stepped onto the field of Yankee Stadium, awed by the magnificence of the ballpark and 65,000 of the noisiest fans in the baseball world. I was a thirteen-year-old kid from a South Bronx neighborhood who through the kindly intercession of his big brother had become the batboy for the New York Yankees.

It was April 1949. The New York season opened with an exhibition game between the Yankees and the Brooklyn Dodgers. I was alone and scared, sitting on an equipment locker in the visitor's clubhouse waiting for the game to start when a player came over to me and said in a soft voice, "Opening day jitters, son. Go get yourself a Coke and put it on my bill. It's going to be okay."

Jackie Robinson seemed to know how I was feeling. But after I drank the Coke and talked to Jackie for a minute, my anxieties melted away. I stuffed the empty Coke bottle in my back pocket and took the field.

Like nearly every boy in America, I wanted to be a major league ballplayer. And for as long as I could remember, there was only one team in the universe that really mattered to me – the New York Yankees.

When I started with the team in 1949, it seemed that my dreams had come true. Here I was in the same locker room with the world's greatest baseball ballplayers. I was even allowed by my principal to leave school at noon for the afternoon games. He had a condition for this privilege, though. He told me to spend my time at Yankee Stadium talking to and observing baseball's greatest players.

"Find out the secrets of their success, Joe. Learn everything you can from them. This is the chance of a lifetime."

Jackie Robinson was one of many great ballplayers, who, in my seven years with the Yankees, helped ease my transition to the adult world. As I sat and thought about Terrence, I heard the echo of voices from years gone by.

"Be persistent," said Jackie on another occasion. "Don't ever give up. That's been the secret of my success."

"Concentrate – focus," said Joe Page, the Yankees' ace relief pitcher.

"When you're half the size of those big strong guys, try twice as hard," said the diminutive shortstop Phil Rizzuto.

"Set your goals. Don't get distracted," said Bobby "Doc" Brown, the Yankees' third baseman, who played baseball and studied medicine at the same time.

"Be shrewd. Exploit every opportunity," said Frank Crosetti, the Yankees' third base coach.

"Think about everything that can happen before it happens," said Ted Williams of the feared Boston Red Sox.

"Stay interested. There's always more to learn," said the last American hero, Joe DiMaggio.

Synchronicity. The fortuitous occurrence of events. It's a word used to describe the good fortune that brought me within the orbit of some of the greatest Yankee teams of all time. I was there from 1949 to 1953 when the Yankees won an unprecedented, still unsurpassed five consecutive World Series.

And it was synchronicity that brought together the wisdom and experience of Joe DiMaggio and the electrifying power of Mickey Mantle. As Joe Di took his final bow, the youthful Mick lit the Stadium like a shooting star.

And it was synchronicity that I was there – in the courtroom for Terrence. For the lessons of all those years with the Yankees were not lost on me as I stood to address the court. Because persistence, and concentration, and goals had all played a part in protecting the life of young Terrence. But more than that, it was memories of the kindness of players such as Jackie Robinson, Phil Rizzuto, and Joe DiMaggio that gave form and meaning to what I was about to say. It was the memory of an adult world that knew its obligations to protect and nurture its children, of players who, though far from perfect, would never knowingly let a kid down. And, in my words, I hoped to do proud the tradition of Yankee greatness that would always be a part of my life.

As I rose to speak, I remembered the words of the great Dodgers' catcher, Roy Campanella.

"Say a prayer before you start. Don't pray that you win the game. Just pray that you get out there and be the best you can."

I didn't want the court to consider the law. The judges knew the law. I wanted the court to hear the facts. I wanted them to focus on the plight of a nine-year-old child who, but for our intervention, would be thrown back to an adult world that nearly destroyed him. I pleaded that he be given a chance – a chance that every child deserved – a chance to live his life and make something of it. He wasn't going to have that chance unless we made it for him.

As I built to my closing argument, the courtroom was hushed. "If the government is allowed to take this child to Zimbabwe, it will have taken the body of a little boy, but it will never capture his soul or his spirit."

My words seemed to crystallize for the newspapers and

television cameras what this case was really about. Although by a 2 to 1 vote, Judge Weinstein's order was upheld, the tide had turned. The State Department, which had pursued this case relentlessly, was backing off. The scrutiny of cameras and bright lights were more than it could handle. The government was looking for a graceful way out and agreed to what Dr. Gries sought from the beginning – a therapeutic transfer. Terrence would leave the good care of St. Christopher's when he felt he was ready to go. We had won.

After more phone calls and interviews than I can possibly remember, I returned to my home late that night. My wife and children were fast asleep when I went into my den and there unlocked a cabinet. And from the shelf inside, I removed an old Coke bottle. It was dusty, but otherwise none the worse for wear. I took a cloth, rubbed it clean, and as I sat and fingered the bottle, I remembered all I had seen, and heard, and learned from the great ballplayers of my childhood days. And in remembering, I resolved to retell – for my children and any who would care to listen – my story. The story of a young boy from a New York neighborhood whose childhood memories are filled with the words and deeds of DiMaggio, Berra, Robinson, and so many others. It's about lessons I learned that gave form and substance to my life, lessons that have lasted a lifetime and that, for me, have made all the difference.

2

Swing from the heels

I was born in the South Bronx and grew up there in the 1940s and '50s. As a kid, I couldn't imagine a better place to live and play than Lincoln Avenue. In a neighborhood bustling with life, I had lots of friends and a family that loved me. Everything I wanted or needed was within walking distance, from the candy store on 136th Street to the baseball fields at Harvey's Hill Park.

The most fascinating part of my old neighborhood, though, was its proximity to Yankee Stadium. Barely a mile away, the Stadium drew us like a magnet and provided a connection to the larger but little understood world beyond our Bronx backyard.

I knew the Yankees as well as I did my best friends. In those days, I'd sit with my mom and dad, my brother Ralph and listen to Mel Allen on the Philco radio as he described every exploit of Joe DiMaggio, Yogi Berra, Allie Reynolds, Joe Page, and Charlie Keller. We spoke about these players with a familiarity born of love and admiration. They were the latest representatives of a proud tradition, rooted in a glorious past, and symbolic of a hope-filled future. And they belonged to us.

I still remember the day in 1948 that Babe Ruth died. I was playing stickball with my friends on 134th Street. From one of the open windows in a nearby tenement someone shouted that the Babe had passed away. In disbelief, and with tears in our eyes, we asked each other, "How could a hero die?" We stopped playing and went home to quietly mourn the passing of one of the great inspirations of our early lives.

Later in life we realized that Babe Ruth was more than a hero. He was a legend, and legends never die.

Like my friends, I loved baseball and I was obsessed with the people who played it. But unlike them, I was permitted a very extraordinary experience, spending seven years of my young life in the Yankee clubhouse as a Yankee ballboy and batboy.

I was really just an average kid in an average New York neighborhood in the late 1940s. What were my odds on becoming the Yankee batboy? One in a million, I guess, except that the odds improved considerably because my brother Ralph was the Yankee ballboy before me. It all started very improbably. One summer day in 1946, when I was ten, Ralph and I were playing baseball with some friends in Macombs Dam Park, which is directly across from Yankee Stadium. Among the crowd was Harry Jacobs, who had recently become the Yankee batboy. Harry's brother Red was the batboy for the Giants at the Polo Grounds and their father was the groundskeeper there. Ed Butterfield, the Yankee operations manager, must have recognized Harry. He came over to our game, struck up a conversation, and said he was looking for someone to fill the ballboy position since Harry was graduating to batboy. Butterfield took one look at Ralph, asked him a few questions, and then told Ralph to stop by his office the following week. He did, and the rest is history.

The news spread throughout our South Bronx neighborhood like a runaway fire: up and down Lincoln, Alexander, and Willis Avenue, from 134th to 141st Streets, every youngster had heard that one of their own was to be the new ballboy at Yankee Stadium.

On days when the Yankees played an afternoon game, I would wait patiently with my friends for Ralph to alight the train at 138th Street and Lincoln Avenue. Most often, he was carrying a broken bat, an old glove, or a scuffed baseball. These relics were usually distributed among the throngs that followed Ralph home. During the four blocks to our apartment, we peppered him with questions.

"What kind of guy is Joe DiMaggio?"

"How big is Phil Rizzuto?"

"Do you play with them?"

And Ralph said, "Of course I play with them."

Then he added in a deadly earnest tone, "Joe DiMaggio is the greatest player that ever lived."

We would get chills when Ralph would speak about Joe Di springing like a cat at the crack of the bat, effortlessly making a put out, or swinging his bat in a split second as he connected for a long home run.

In those pre-television years, my family often spent the evenings in awe-filled silence listening to Ralph's stories about Yankee stars like George Stirnweiss, Tommy Henrich, Vic Raschi, and Allie Reynolds. Ralph had become a neighborhood celebrity and it was magnificent to see the crowds part on Lincoln Avenue on the afternoon of a night game when he brought home Frank Shea, the Yankee pitcher. Ralph had promised this Irishman one of Mom Carrieri's spaghetti dinners. Frank really seemed to enjoy Mom's home-made raviolis in red sauce. We shuddered, though, when he told us he was used to having raviolis covered with milk or butter.

Although I never articulated it, I'm sure that somewhere deep inside me a hope was born that I, too, might find a role with the New York Yankees. But I was too young or shy to ever ask my brother to put in a word for me and was content to share in his glory. However, at the end of the 1948 season, Ralph came home from the Stadium one day, put his arm around me, and said, "Joe, how'd you like to work at Yankee Stadium?"

"Are you kidding," I answered, "I'd love to work at Yankee Stadium."

I was only twelve and I didn't have any idea what the job would be. I thought he would probably try to get me a job selling peanuts, ice cream or scorecards. But that would've been fine because I would be able to watch the games for free, see the players up close, and have a shot at meeting Joe DiMaggio.

Ralph said, "Good. Next Saturday I'm going to introduce you to Pete Sheehy."

I couldn't believe my ears. Sheehy was the clubhouse man – the one in charge of hiring ballboys and batboys.

In October, shortly after the end of the baseball season, Ralph and I walked the twenty-seven blocks to the Stadium at 161st Street and River Avenue. It was and is a magnificent baseball cathedral and I can still remember that childhood feeling as it came into view that day, half-whispering to myself, "I'm gonna take the field at Yankee Stadium. I'm gonna be a New York Yankee." It was really a too-good-to-be-true moment, like the unrestrained excitement you feel when you get the present you always wanted but in a million years never expected to receive.

Joe Serrano, the doorman, opened the office door, flashed a grin at Ralph and said, "Who's this little guy?"

"My kid brother. I'm trying to get him a job as visiting batboy."

"What happened to Gallagher?"

"He joined the Marines," answered Ralph, as Joe let us in. "We're going to talk to Pete."

"You know where he is?" Serrano asked.

"Same place he always is, I guess."

"That's right."

We travelled through a labyrinth of walkways, then down a flight of cement stairs to a red-carpeted area in front of a red door with a sign YANKEE CLUBHOUSE.

It was quiet inside the room as we entered. The players had long since taken their equipment and headed for home. Sheehy seemed to know that I was coming. He was sitting at a big picnic table, but got up as soon as we walked in. He was wearing a tee-shirt, chinos, and black oxfords with no socks. When I first met him, Sheehy was about 45 years old, 5'8", with a ruddy complexion and brown hair combed straight back.

"Well, you're Ralph's brother," he said putting his arm around my shoulder. "Welcome aboard."

Then he grabbed a pile of clothes off the picnic table and handed me a gray shirt and pants, a Yankee cap, white socks, and blue stirrups. What I thought might be a tough interview was transformed by Pete into a quick affirmation that I had the job. My heart stopped pounding.

Sheehy seemed genuinely glad of the company. The place was awfully quiet. I tried to imagine what the clubhouse must be like on game days, with players, reporters, photographers bustling, joking, laughing, teasing. My brother left to talk to Ed Butterfield for a few moments, and Sheehy started right in, telling me that he had been the clubhouse man long before

I was born – 1928, to be exact.

"Then you knew Babe Ruth?" I asked.

"Of course I did," said Sheehy. "Nobody loved baseball more than the Babe."

"He was the greatest home run hitter, ever, wasn't he?"

"That he was," said Sheehy. "The greatest home run hitter and the king of strikeouts."

Why did Pete want to cut the Babe down like that, I wondered to myself. Before I could ask him though, my brother was back and the two of them offered to give me the grand tour.

The Yankee clubhouse room was spacious, about 45 x 100 feet. In the middle of it as you walked in, there were three picnic tables with benches. Directly in back of the tables were the players' lockers. Behind the lockers, at the far end of the clubhouse, was a trainer's room with a whirlpool, a rubbing table, stacks of gauze tape and pharmaceutical paraphernalia. Next to the trainer's room was a utility room with a washer and dryer. The manager's office was off to the left as you walked in. It had a big wooden desk, a couch, and several chairs. On the opposite side was a spacious shower room and, next to it, a large area with a dozen sinks and mirrors. The locker room smelled both sweet and stale, a combination of men's cologne, cigarette smoke, and beer.

The clubhouse didn't have metal lockers as I expected; instead, each player had a wooden cubicle that gave him his own 4 x 4 foot room. To me, it seemed luxurious – grander by far than any locker room I had ever seen. The cubicles went all the way to the ceiling with hangers and shelves for the players' uniforms and street clothes. A high shelf housed their gloves, baseballs, and other personal items.

After the tour, Sheehy said, "You can leave that uniform here...or, if you want, you can take it home and ask your mom to wash and iron it before opening day."

"I'll bring it home," I answered, not wanting to let the uniform slip out of my hands.

Sheehy whispered to Ralph, but, I'm sure, loud enough so that I could hear, "Ralph, if he's half as good as you, he'll make a great batboy."

We took the subway home and when we arrived at our tenement on Lincoln Avenue, all my friends were there to meet me.

"Did you really get the job, Joe?" they all wanted to know. I just opened my bag. In no time, Bobby Corbo was wearing my Yankee hat and Billy Seidel was trying on my shirt.

I hardly went inside for the rest of the weekend. I sat on the stoop in front of our apartment looking for familiar faces, just in case there was some passing acquaintance who hadn't heard my good news.

On Monday, as usual, I went to St. Jerome's Grammar School, a few blocks from home on 136th Street, between Alexander and Willis Avenues. The whole school was abuzz about my good fortune. My excitement was short-lived, however. Shortly after classes started, I was summoned to the principal's office.

In 1948, being summoned solo to the principal's office produced that sweaty palms, fear in the heart, "Why me and what did I do" feeling. In this situation, rule one said expect the worst and you won't be disappointed. I slithered out of my desk as I saw my dreams of Yankee glory going up in smoke.

In the late 1940s, major league baseball teams played fewer games at night and many more in the afternoon. In fact, the

Yankees didn't play their first game under the Stadium lights until 1946. In the euphoria of the prior Saturday, I hadn't considered that my principal, Brother Colombo, stood between me and my dreams of Yankee glory. If I was to be the Yankee batboy, I had to be at the Stadium, in uniform, on-time, ready to work; which meant that I had to leave school early in the spring and fall.

I had no idea what Brother Colombo would do. He was fair, but strict. This was one path my brother Ralph couldn't clear for me. He was already in high school when he started his job at Yankee Stadium. In my imagination, I could hear Brother saying, "Joe, school's more important than being the Yankee batboy. You're here to get an education." I'm sure my parents would have agreed with him. After I arrived, he began, with a poker face, "Denis Dillon told me you've been offered a job with the Yankees next spring."

"Dillon, the rat!" I said to myself.

But then Brother Colombo smiled and said, "I suppose you'll want to leave school early for the afternoon games. You know, Joe, don't you, that's against the rules."

Before I could answer, he said, "Joe, I love the game of baseball. I think this is a great opportunity for you and I wouldn't want you to miss it. You can make the afternoon home games on two conditions: first, you have to maintain a B+ in all your subjects; if you don't, then the deal is off; second, you have to turn your time at Yankee Stadium into a learning experience. You have a good opportunity to discover why some players succeed where others fail. I want you to find out the secrets of their success."

Before I could get a word in, Brother was off again.

"You know, Joe, I used to watch Babe Ruth play at the

Stadium. He was the greatest hitter I ever saw. He swung from the heels every time. That's how he hit so many home runs."

"But he struck out a lot too, didn't he Brother?"

Without either of us noticing the transition, we were no longer principal and student, but just two people with an immeasurable love for the game.

He answered just like one of my friends, "You gotta take risks, Joe. He could've played it safe. But he didn't. To be the greatest home run hitter, he had to take the big cuts. He had to swing from the heels."

And with a smile, I remembered my conversation with Sheehy the previous Saturday. Now I understood what he meant. The sultan of swat was destined to be the king of strike-outs.

"So, you've got your assignment."

"Yes Brother. I've got it."

"Okay. So I want you to come back from time to time and tell me…"

"What makes Joe DiMaggio great?"

"Right. And Charlie Keller and Phil Rizzuto…and anyone else. It's up to you. Let's see what you find out. And then let's see what you can do with it."

"Got it, Brother."

"Good luck. Now get back to class."

19

3

Someone's always watching

In my old neighborhood, there was virtually no crime. People walked the street, day or night, without fear. Whether we wanted to or not, we traded privacy for safety; the closeness of tenement life made us take the everyday for granted; we hardly noticed our neighbors, but instantly recognized a stranger.

Although we lived on the third floor of a four-story tenement, during the day our apartment door was not only unlocked, it was usually half opened. Neighbors felt free to politely knock on the door and come right into our kitchen for a cup of tea or coffee. Edna May and Eleanor, who had apartments below ours, came by nearly every afternoon for a chat with Mom and to enjoy some of her home-made apple pie or pound cake. Mom never felt put out by this – she was too good-natured for that. But there was an element of self-interest to her kindness. In my South Bronx neighborhood, there was an unwritten rule that if you looked out for other people, they looked out for you and yours. Like any good mom, she guarded her prized possessions, Ralph and me, and knew that if she wasn't there, Edna May or Eleanor wouldn't let her down.

My brother Ralph was the north star of this safe, secure universe. He made sure that I was included in baseball or basketball games with his friends who, being three or four years older, naturally regarded me as a nuisance. For many years, we shared the same small bedroom in our Lincoln Avenue apartment. Aside from some books, a crucifix, and my plants, the room was from end to end a shrine to Yankee glory. Banners, pennants, team pictures, and autographed baseballs, bats and gloves memorialized the best years of Ralph's life.

The winter of 1948-49 seemed endless – moreso for Ralph, I'm sure, who endured my endless questioning. After finishing up homework and maybe listening to a boxing match on the Philco, we hit the sack and then my barrage began.

"Who makes up the batting order?"

"Who's the new manager?"

"Do you think I can become the Yankee batboy someday?"

"How much money does the visiting batboy make?"

"Joe Di's coming back next year, isn't he?"

And Ralph would answer:

"The manager."

"Casey Stengel."

"Yeah, you can become Yankee batboy when I retire," he said with a laugh.

"A dollar a day."

"How many times do I have to tell you...Joe Di *is* coming back."

In retrospect, it's not surprising that he actually answered most of these questions. He was a master with an eager apprentice and he finally had someone to share his passion with – someone who was learning to love and admire the Yankees as much as he did.

About two weeks before the opening day of the 1949 season, my excitement probably more than even my big brother could any longer tolerate, Ralph decided we should check-in at the Stadium. Although the Yankees were playing in the Florida sunshine, Ralph thought that on a blustery day in March we should locate our lockers, catch up with Pete Sheehy and company, and let the Yankee establishment know that we were alive, well, and ready to go. Besides, Ralph had grown a lot in the past year and wanted to make sure that he had a new uniform before opening day.

Admonishing Ralph, "Take good care of Joey," Mom gave us the fare for the subway – ten cents each way – insisting that "you walk and you'll be sick for opening day." Mom always knew what buttons to push. We didn't mind the walk and would usually save the fare for better things.

As we walked up to 138th Street to catch the subway, I turned near the end of the block and saw Mom following us as far as her eyes would permit. She waved as we rounded the corner. I glanced back, gave her my best smile, and headed eagerly toward my future.

When we arrived at the clubhouse, Joe Serrano opened wide the clubhouse door as he had the previous October, greeted Ralph, and said "Well, Joe, you're official now." I nodded and smiled, feeling quite important. As we walked through the clubhouse, I saw Pete Sheehy getting things ready for the return of the Yankees. Sheehy introduced me to Pete Previte, the assistant clubhouse man, who was in charge of selling soda, beer, sandwiches, chewing tobacco, cigarettes, gum and candy to the Yankee players. It was also his responsibility to shine shoes and, generally, help Sheehy in any way required. To avoid confusion, Sheehy was known as "Big Pete"; Previte, who was considerably smaller, was known as "Little Pete."

Both Petes were busy shining shoes and hanging up pin-striped uniforms in the players' cubicles. Unlike my previous meeting with Sheehy, this time he was preoccupied, getting ready for the return of the Yankees from spring training.

"Hey Joe, let's go," said Pete. "You're the batboy for the visiting teams. Ralph, take him over and introduce him to George."

Before I had time to say a word, I was getting what seemed like a mini-lecture from Pete.

"Remember Joe, nobody likes a fresh kid. Whenever someone asks you to do something, never, ever say no. Even if you think you can't do it, try. At least the player will know you gave it your best effort. Remember, from now on thousands of people are going to be watching what you do."

"Just let me put a few things in my locker," said Ralph, "before we head over to the other clubhouse."

I was a little taken aback by Pete. I looked longingly, jealously, and anxiously at Ralph's four by four foot locker, just like the ones all the other Yankees had. Not only was I being separated from the security I felt with Ralph, I was going to be sharing space with Cleveland Indians and Washington Senators – not the New York Yankees.

Ralph took me over to meet George Natriano, who was in charge of the visiting clubhouse. We navigated the tunnels beneath the Stadium and when we reached the visiting clubhouse, Natriano was straightening things up, stacking soda, beer, and pretzels and airing the place out.

He knew I was coming and greeted me warmly. "Okay, Joe. Good to see you. Always glad to have an extra pair of hands. Let's get you situated."

George was in his 60s, short, dark, with a big nose. He was affectionately known around the clubhouse as the Greek. After Natriano showed me my locker, which was much smaller than Ralph's, he gave me the rundown on my responsibilities.

"Try and get here about two hours before game time. There's always lots to do. You have to bring the bats into the dugout before the game. Get the scorecard from the manager or a coach as soon as you can. That'll give you the lineup. Once you have that, you'll know what order the bats should be in and you can put them in the right slot in the bat rack located at the edge of the dugout. For the guys that aren't playing, you just make sure their bat is out there but not in any particular order."

George also told me that if I wanted I could go in the outfield during batting practice and shag fly balls. I was also on call to run to a local store to buy oranges or get a player his favorite malted. But my primary responsibility was to make sure that I handed the right bat to each player as he approached the on-deck circle and to retrieve the bat as soon as it left the batter's hand, particularly if it was in a runner's path.

The less glamorous part of the job included shining shoes and picking up dirty laundry dropped by the players.

After about an hour of stacking and cleaning, Natriano told me to call it a day. On the way out, he put his arm around me and said, "Joe, Ralph is very well liked here at Yankee Stadium by the workers, players, and management. He vouched for you and that's good enough for us. Don't let Ralph down."

Ralph's shadow had always protected me. Now it was something I had to measure up to. And all those fans at Yankee Stadium, whose eyes might just fix their gaze on me. I now realized that being visiting batboy, while exciting and fun, had responsibilities. As I made my way back through the underground tunnels, I vowed that I would learn as much as I possibly could about each player, about which was his practice bat and which his game bat.

When I got back to the Yankee clubhouse, things had settled down a bit and I found a quiet place to wait for Ralph.

"Kind of overwhelming, isn't it?" said Sheehy, who sneaked up on me.

"If I was your age, can't think of a place I'd rather be."

"I can hardly believe I'm really here," I said.

"Look," Pete said with a smile, "I stay in the clubhouse where I belong. I just have to worry about pleasing these twenty-five guys and my boss. But you're out there in front of the crowd. So how you handle yourself reflects – on the Yankees and on you. Remember that. It's something every guy in pinstripes has to remember."

"Pete was right. If you dropped a fly, muffed a grounder, or struck out, the fans were going to let you know about it. And they could be fickle and unforgiving. I was a fan. I knew from experience.

"At that moment, Ralph came along in his pinstripes. It was a perfect fit and he looked great. As I looked at him, I had a mixed sensation. It was the first time in my life that I was conscious of passing from one world to another. Now I had to stand on my own. No one else could do it for me. But as I looked at Ralph in his Yankee pinstripes, I felt I could do it...if for no other reason, because I wanted to wear the Yankee uniform more than anything else in the world.

4

Opening Day

It was early April 1949. My first day on the job. My heart was pounding and I was excited beyond belief. Here I was, thirteen years old, born in the South Bronx, amidst some of the greatest baseball players that ever lived. The New York Yankees were to take on the Brooklyn Dodgers in a pre-season exhibition game.

Both Ralph and I cut classes and flew to Yankee Stadium. Ralph's parting instructions were "Just stay alert. Pay attention to George...and if Mr. Shotton tells you to do anything, do it on the double."

I checked in with George Natriano in the visitor's clubhouse, put on my gray uniform, got the Dodgers scorecard from Burt Shotton, the Dodgers' manager, and started stacking the bats in the slots where they belonged. On this first day, George checked everything I did.

About a half-hour before the game, I perched atop an equipment locker and unwrapped the pepper and egg sandwich that my mom had prepared for me. I was anxious about the job I had to do, hoping that I would do everything right and not quite knowing how to approach the baseball players I was here to serve. No sooner had I bit into the sandwich than I was overshadowed by a tall player in a Dodgers' uniform.

"Son, your sandwich looks dry. Why don't you get a soda

and put it on my bill."

I was star-struck; dumbfounded. He came a bit closer and said again, "Son, take a soda, and put it on my bill."

Despite all the sage advice I received from Ralph and Pete Sheehy about responding promptly to players, I sat there. Gil Hodges, observing what had been going on, came over, put his hand on my shoulder and said, "Jackie Robinson wants to buy you a Coke."

Finally, I jumped up and went over to the soda cooler with Jackie. He picked out a seven ounce bottle, flipped the cap and handed it to me. I thanked him profusely and nodded to Gil Hodges, and then, I consumed with pleasure the pepper and egg sandwich my mother had made, washing it down with a Coke bought for me by Jackie Robinson.

About five minutes to game time, the Dodgers bolted from the clubhouse, stampeding through the runway and into the dugout. I stood in awe as Duke Snider, Carl Furillo, Pee Wee Reese, Roy Campanella, Billy Cox and Ralph Branca ran past me.

As I was about to man my post at the on-deck circle, Natriano tapped me on the shoulder and said, "Oh, Joe, I forgot to mention something to you. Charlie DiGiovanna, the Dodgers' batboy is here tonight. So he'll be taking over."

Charlie must have seen my face because he immediately said, "No George. I'm resting up tonight. Let Joe do the honors."

The visiting Dodgers were up first. Quickly, Pee Wee Reese was on first with a walk. Jackie Robinson singled to right center as he did so often, sending Reese to third; Jackie made his patented long turn at first and then quickly returned to the bag. With a man on first, Vic Raschi was pitching from the stretch. On a 2 and 2 count, Raschi's fastball was low and outside and

Jackie Robinson was on the move. Yogi Berra made a clean catch, crouched, cocked his arm...and never threw the ball. It wouldn't even have been close. With the stolen base, there was a tremendous roar. Jackie Robinson had sparked the imagination of the New York crowd and it was obvious that he was winning the hearts of Yankee fans – natural enemies of the feared Brooklyn Dodgers. Although, I was through and through a Yankee fan, as a recent beneficiary of Jackie Robinson's kindness and attention, I couldn't help but cheer for him.

The Dodgers won 3 to 2. As they munched their sandwiches and soaked down sodas and beers in the clubhouse, they laughed and joked as they dissected every play of the game.

Meanwhile, a huge man with a hearty laugh dressed in a Dodgers uniform nearly knocked the players aside as he ambled up to Charlie DiGiovanna and said, "Hey Charlie, how 'bout doing the post-game show."

Happy Felton was a Dodgers institution, for years filling every inch of those prehistoric television screens as he interviewed players, managers, or fans while doing the pre- and post-game television shows.

"I had the day off, Happy. How about interviewing the new batboy, Joe Carrieri."

Happy said "Sure," and before I knew what was happening, he took me by the arm, through the dugout, onto the field, and in front of the television camera.

Happy introduced me to the television audience, which at that time probably numbered only in the thousands. He was completely at ease in front of the camera.

"I'm talking with Joe Carrieri, the batboy for the visiting teams here at Yankee Stadium. You know Joe, you're one of the luckiest kids I can imagine. Do you know how many youngsters would love to be the batboy here at Yankee Stadium. I understand that this is your first day on the job. Why not tell our audience how you became the Yankee batboy?"

"Well, really, through my big brother Ralph, who's the Yankee ballboy. See, he knew Harry Jacobs, who worked at the Stadium...," and I recited him for the synchronicity of good fortune which included my brother Ralph, Red and Harry Jacobs, and Ralph's chance meeting with Ed Butterfield in Macombs Dam Park.

"How old are you?" Happy asked.

"Thirteen."

"What grade are you in?"

"Seventh."

"Where?"

"St. Jerome's on 136th Street in the Bronx."

"And how do you get out of school to get to the afternoon games?"

"Well, I have an agreement with my principal, Brother Colombo. As long as I get B pluses in all my classes and do a special assignment, he'll let me out of school at 12 so I can make the afternoon games."

"And who's your favorite team?"

"The New York Yankees."

"And who's your favorite player?"

"Joe DiMaggio."

"Well, considering you're a Yankee fan, how did it feel to be the batboy for the Dodgers?"

"The Dodgers are a swell bunch of guys and they made me feel at home right off, especially Jackie Robinson and the

Dodgers' batboy Charlie DiGiovanna.

"What did those guys do?" Happy asked.

"Well, Jackie bought me a soda before the game and Charlie could've done this interview but let me do it instead. They're really great guys and now I know why the Dodgers have such loyal fans."

After the interview was finished, Happy gave me a Rawlings glove and a box of chocolate bars, complimentary gifts for appearing on the show. I went back to the visiting clubhouse, showered, and was getting ready to go share my beginner's luck with Ralph when Charlie DiGiovanna came over. "Joe, Jackie would like to see you," he said.

Jackie asked me to sit down and he spoke in the softest voice, but with the utmost sincerity.

"Joe, I heard from Charlie what you told Happy during your interview… that I made you feel comfortable and welcome. Well, that's good because I know what it's like to be a rookie and on the job for the first time."

I sat and listened in reverent silence.

"I'll never forget how nervous I was when I was starting out with the Dodgers. In the second inning, an easy ground ball came my way at second base and I muffed it. I felt terrible but there was no place to hide. In the fifth, another routine ground ball was hit to my left, but I felt paralyzed. I just couldn't get over there in time… and when I did, the ball went right through my legs. I felt so awkward and alone. And then, in front of 50,000 fans, Pee Wee Reese called time, came over to me, put his hand on my shoulder. He just told me to relax. Said I would be a great ballplayer. Everything would be fine. Just relax. After that second error, I was ready to quit. But Pee Wee's kindness and encouragement probably saved my career. So, the best I can do is to pass that kindness along too. You're a rookie, Joe, but you're going make it."

Jackie then reached in his pocket and slowly pulled a five from a wad of bills.

"Here, son. I want you to take this," he said, handing the bill to me.

"Gee, Jackie. Thanks."

"Okay, Joe. We'll see you next time. Be good."

I was in a daze as I made my way out of the visiting clubhouse and through the underground tunnels. But I had to get back and tell Ralph all that had happened my first night on the job.

When I arrived in the Yankee clubhouse, I didn't expect the place to be filled with Yankee uniforms – not, that is, with the players still in them. When I left the visiting clubhouse, everyone but George Natriano had vanished. What I learned later from Ralph is that the visitors get out of the clubhouse as quickly as possible. They're in a hurry to get on the team bus and make their next destination – either back to the hotel or on to the next town. But the home team feels, well...at home. Being in spacious, more luxurious surroundings, they tend to relax and take their time about leaving.

I was a new face in the crowd and none of the Yankees knew me. The clubhouse was off-limits to everyone except players, the clubhouse employees, and the bat and ballboys. Some reporters were allowed in for interviews, but strangers were ushered out in a hurry.

Ralph finally saw me, came over, put his arm around me, and said, "Come on, let's meet some of the guys."

In a blur, I was introduced to George Stirnweiss, Yogi Berra, Vic Raschi, and Allie Reynolds. Most simply said something like "Welcome aboard kid," or "So you're Ralph's brother." Phil Rizzuto, always more colorful and engaging, stood right in my face and said, "Hey, finally, I'm bigger than somebody else in a uniform." He had about an inch on me.

At 5'6", Phil was the smallest player on the Yankees, and probably the smallest player in baseball. But what a classy shortstop. This very day, he went deep in the hole between short and third, gloved the ball, jumped in the air like a ballet dancer, and threw a strike to first, nipping the runner by half a foot.

Phil was the friendliest Yankee I met on my first day at the Stadium and he lived up to Ralph's billing. During our winter talks, Ralph filled me in on all the players. He said that Phil would spend hours talking to just about anyone he would meet at the Stadium; he'd start with the clubhouse staff, move on to the groundskeepers, and as gametime approached he'd chat with the ushers, vendors, and the fans.

"What kind of guys are those Brooklyn Dodgers?" Phil asked.

"Oh, they're real friendly. They talked a lot after the game, saying how good the Yankees are."

I was so afraid of saying the wrong thing, but as time would teach me, it was almost impossible to say the wrong thing to Phil Rizzuto. It struck me that Phil, who was so down to earth, would have fit in perfectly with the Dodgers.

I started to feel a bit more relaxed as a bunch of players I hadn't met, finally realizing that I was Ralph's brother, gathered round and started to pepper me with questions about the Dodgers. "What was Duke Snider saying about his big hit? How'd they think Ebbets Field stacked up to Yankee Stadium?"

But sooner or later, all questions came back to the same subject. "What's Jackie Robinson like? What did Jackie Robinson have to say about us Yankees?"

Jackie Robinson's mere presence on the field represented a sea change in the great American pastime. In the world I grew up in, there were few people of color. To me, integration meant that Irish and Italian kids were attending the same parochial school for the first time.

During the game, I watched the Yankees closely to see how they would react to Jackie. I sensed their keen interest in him and noted, with pride, the respect they showed for him and his talents.

"Well, I didn't really hear him say anything about the Yankees, exactly," I said. "But he told a story about a time he made a couple of errors when he was first starting out."

"Well, his fielding's gotten a lot better," Charlie Keller said. That night his play had been perfect.

The dignified approach of the 1949 Yankees contrasted sharply to the way many teams and audiences reacted to the first black player in the major leagues. The racial epithets and the vicious slides into second, spikes first, were legendary.

"Jackie also bought me a Coke," I said, proudly displaying my souvenir soda bottle. And he gave me a five dollar tip."

"Well you did real good tonight, son," said Charlie Keller. The players were amused, but I hardly noticed.

"Yeah, it's been a pretty special evening. I even got to go on television with Happy Felton."

"They get both of you on that little screen at the same time," Yogi Berra kidded. Everyone laughed.

I smiled awkwardly. I was still feeling my way, but it was coming more naturally.

"Well, we'll be seeing you around Joe." And the little group broke up as the players found their way back to their lockers.

As I stood watching the players head off in one direction, Ralph spun me around 180 degrees and then motioned toward the back of the clubhouse. With only a towel wrapped around him, Joe DiMaggio came out of the shower; about 6'2", slender, but muscular – with a proud, dignified manner. I noticed that his black hair was beginning to streak with gray as he made his way slowly back to his cubicle. His legs and arms were covered with bruises. He settled into his bench, resting, trying to draw back his strength.

Standing, awe-struck, twenty feet from the greatest living baseball legend...I turned to Ralph and said, "Give me something to write on and a pen, quick."

Fortunately, Ralph, composed and in control, said, "Gimme a break, Joe. That's bush league."

I reined myself in and, reluctantly, took my big brother's advice. The autograph would have to wait for another day.

I walked Ralph back to his locker. He wanted to take a shower before we left so I sat down and relaxed. Just about everybody was out of the clubhouse when Sheehy walked over and said, "Come on, I'll introduce you to Joe."

"Great."

Joe Di was sitting inside his cubicle, resting, glancing at a newspaper when Pete said, "Joe, I'd like you to meet Ralph's younger brother, Joe Carrieri."

Joe slowly put down his paper, extended his long muscular arm, and shook my hand firmly. It was a warm handshake; sincere and friendly. Pete headed back to the training room.

I said, "Hi, Joe. It's a pleasure meeting you."

"Likewise." You know some of the guys were talking that Ralphy's younger brother was going to be the visiting batboy today. I was watching you and I have a bone to pick with you."

"Uh…yeah," I answered, feeling weak in the knees. I couldn't imagine what Joe meant, but I was sure it had to be something important for him to bring it up like this.

"You really shouldn't shake Duke Snider's hand when he hits a home run like you did today if you ever intend to be the Yankee batboy."

I started to relax a little. "Okay, sure, Joe. I'll remember that," I said with a smile. I knew now that this oh-so-serious guy was just kidding me a little. But, really, about the only thing that registered was "if you ever intend to be the Yankee batboy." That was a dream worth dreaming about and here was Joe DiMaggio telling me on my first day at Yankee Stadium that it just might happen.

A small part of the great Yankee tradition included the apprenticeship of ball and batboys. I was on the first rung of the ladder as the visiting batboy. Usually, this person was thirteen or fourteen when he started. As soon as there was an opening, there'd be some upward movement. If the Yankee batboy went away to college, then the ballboy would become the Yankee batboy and the visiting batboy would move up a step to become the ballboy. Since I was only thirteen, I knew if I didn't mess up, I had a shot someday at becoming the Yankee batboy.

35

Not wanting to take up any more of Joe's time, I started to back away and said, "It was real nice seeing you."

Before he could answer, a look of excruciating pain crossed his face and he clutched his calf. I panicked. By the time I came back with the trainer, Gus Mauch, the color was returning to Joe's face. Gus knelt on the floor and started rubbing Joe's calf.

"Just a cramp, Joe" said Gus. "Come on. I'll give you a rub-down and see if we can't relax those muscles."

Joe got slowly up from his stool. Leaning on Gus' shoulder, he hobbled toward the far end of the clubhouse.

As he made his pain-filled exit, I couldn't help but think of the DiMaggio that would live forever in my imagination. DiMaggio who hit in fifty-six straight games; DiMaggio who could run the bases as gracefully as they'd ever been run; DiMaggio who roamed center field as if he owned it. I wanted to know the Joe that had been captured for me in the papers, on the radio, in newsreels at Saturday matinees. That Joe was fading and soon would be gone.

That was my only sad moment my first day at Yankee Stadium; a premonition of autumn on the first day of spring.

Ralph and I wouldn't leave until we knew Joe was all right. The clubhouse air filled with the sweet, heavy smell of liniment. We waited patiently. After a short while, Joe walked back from the trainer's room, limping ever so slightly.

Ralph asked, "You want us to hang around and walk you to your car, Joe."

"Don't bother," he said. I have some friends picking me up. Thanks anyway." Ralph had told me that Joe Di often left the clubhouse with well-known celebrities.

Joe began to dress himself in a dark suit and white shirt,

according to Ralph, his trademark civilian uniform.

We said good night to Pete. When we opened the clubhouse door, we noticed Joe's friends had the car waiting by the exit. It was too dark to tell if it was someone famous.

The night air was cool and crisp. But it had the springy smell of anticipation when you know the green leaves and grass and flower blossoms are only a few days away.

"Hey, Ralph," I said, "it was a great night."

"Couldn't have been much better, that's for sure," he said. "What was your favorite part of the evening?" Joe.

"Jackie Robinson. Most definitely."

"Why's that?"

"Just the way he thought about me. You know…here's one of the greatest guys playing baseball and he buys a Coke for the low man on the roster. Made me feel like I belonged."

Just then we reached the subway entrance. The sign was illuminated by a single light. The street was deserted. The Yankee and Dodgers fans had long since scattered to the far ends of New York City and beyond. We descended the darkened stairs into the dimly lit, nearly empty station.

In just a few minutes, the local arrived and we hopped aboard. The subway carried only a few late night passengers. We settled quietly into a dream-like trance, staring at the blackened windows, focusing on nothing in particular. We said hardly a word, our reverie interrupted only slightly by the pull and push of the train's momentum at each subway stop.

Finally, at Lincoln Avenue, we came up to the lights a couple of blocks from our apartment.

Ralph broke the silence. "The opener's only a few days away."

"I can't wait," I said.

"On opening day," Ralph said, "why don't you go home from St. Jerome's, get your stuff. I'll pick you up by 12:15 and we can get to the Stadium by 12:30."

"That doesn't make any sense, Ralph. You'd have to go way out of your way to get me. It's a lot easier for you to go straight from Cardinal Hayes."

With a surprised look on his face, he said, "I don't mind."

"No. Let's meet at the Stadium," I answered. "I can get there by myself."

"You sure?"

"Absolutely. I'm absolutely sure."

5

Secrets of success

I soon established my working routine. If the Yankees were in town on a school day, I'd leave St. Jerome's at noon, hustle from 136th to 138th Street and the Grand Concourse, hop on the Concourse bus, wolf my sandwich in transit, jump off at 161st Street and run the last two blocks to the Stadium, arriving about 12:30 for a 2:00 start. I'd dash into the clubhouse, check in with George, and in no time at all, I'd change into my gray visitor's uniform.

Once I had the scorecard, I knew how to stack the starters' bats. That done, I'd pile towels at one end of the dugout, help George fold the laundry, and organize the sandwiches and other items that he would sell to the players. If it was a chilly day, I'd lug two heavy urns of hot bouillon into the dugout to keep the visiting players warm. When my pre-game chores were completed, I'd sprint to the outfield to shag fly balls. I did all this before my real job as the visiting batboy began.

This was work – my first real experience of exchanging my time and energy for the stuff that makes the world go round. Although I was tired when I arrived home at 6:30 or 7:00, I liked the deal.

I was soon glad to be in the visitor's clubhouse. That's how I earned my daily bread. Meeting Ted Williams of the Red Sox or Bob Feller of the Cleveland Indians was a bonus – the real pay was a dollar a game, two for doubleheaders. After a homestand, I was paid three or four dollars by one of the visiting coaches. I could also take my compensation in the form of one American League baseball for each game I worked.

Early in the 1949 season, I was more than happy to take three or four baseballs when the visitors were about to leave town. They came in handy for baseball games at Harvey's Hill, a neighborhood park. Besides, baseballs had a way of going – down a sewer, over a fence, or through a window – and never coming back.

I wasn't long into this practice of taking my pay in baseballs when Frank Crosetti, the Yankees' third base coach and custodian of the Yankee baseballs, grabbed me.

"Hey Joe," he said, "I hear them visiting coaches are paying you in baseballs. Don't do that no more," he said with a note of irritated paternal concern.

"You work hard for your money. Whenever you need a baseball, come see me."

I took Frank up on his offer and soon learned a lesson in thrift and enterprise. If I got Frank Crosetti's baseballs autographed by the Yankees, I could easily double or triple my weekly salary by selling them to an usher or scorecard vendor for five dollars a ball. They had no trouble selling them to eager fans for a lot more than that. With Ralph's help from inside the Yankee clubhouse, I was usually able to get two autographed balls a week. In no time, the dollar-a-day batboy was earning about ten dollars extra a week. This was more than lunch money and I finally understood what it meant to have your cake and eat it too.

Besides the Yankees, there were only seven teams in the American League in 1949: the Cleveland Indians; the Boston Red Sox; the Philadelphia Athletics; the St. Louis Browns; the Chicago White Sox; the Detroit Tigers; and the Washington Senators. My two favorite visiting teams were the Boston Red Sox and the Cleveland Indians. I particularly liked the Red Sox because of Ted Williams. In my pantheon of stars, Ted ranked in the upper galactic reaches, just below Joe DiMaggio. In fact, I thought of him as a left-handed Joe Di.

They both had great natural ability. They were built similarly. Ted was tall, about 6'2", and strong, weighing in at around 195 pounds. Like Joe Di, he had long muscles in his arms. But Ted's extraordinary eyesight was renowned and probably unique in all of baseball.

I remember a summer Saturday in 1949 when Ted amazed everyone during batting practice, saying, "Home plate's off. It's not in the right spot."

Ted, who was kind of quiet and introspective, and was known for his irritability, drew some amazed stares.

"It's off," he insisted.

Well, this was a first. Home plate was a fixed point in the universe and no other player, Yankee or visitor, had ever done anything but adjust his position and stance relative to this immovable object and take his swings.

But Ted wasn't giving an inch. Looking at me, he barked, "Go get the groundskeeper. I want him to measure it."

I knew how to take an order. I ran immediately to the groundskeepers' pen.

"Ted Williams says home base is off. He wants you guys to come measure it."

I was showered with enough "Get outta here's" (expletives deleted) for a lifetime.

"Ted Williams won't take another swing until one of you guys comes out," I insisted.

Ted Williams being Ted Williams, Walter Owens the head groundskeeper soon came. By this time, a crowd had gathered. When the measurements were taken, the groundskeeper uttered, "I don't believe it." But it was true. Home plate was off a fraction of an inch. It was unearthed, readjusted, and Ted, satisfied, ignoring the disbelieving throng, resumed his batting practice.

Ted Williams' temperament was different from Joe DiMaggio's. Where Joe was subdued, Ted was distant and unapproachable. Neither was personable like a Phil Rizzuto, but both filled a room with their presence. They had some unnamed quality. Call it charisma. When they talked, which wasn't often, people listened.

But I was dying to know what made Ted tick. Besides, I was a young man with a mission. After all, hadn't Brother Colombo told me to find out why some players succeed where others fail. Well, he was one of the two most successful men in baseball – the last one to hit .400 and one of the all-time great home run hitters.

Since each visiting team made about five trips to Yankee Stadium in a season, by about the fourth trip I had worked up the courage to approach him.

"Ted," I said before the start of a night game, "I'm doing a school report about great baseball players. I picked you as the subject. Can you spare a few minutes for a couple of questions."

I figured that even the occasionally irritable Ted Williams couldn't turn down such a request.

"Not now, Joe," was his curt response. "See me after the game."

It was better than a flat "no"; besides, I wasn't easily discouraged.

The Red Sox won that one and Ted had a good game, hitting a double and a home run. As I did my post game chores, I could tell he was feeling pretty good. I decided to talk to him again but waited until he had showered and was enjoying a beer.

When I finally approached him, he said, "What were you trying to do before, Joe, break my concentration?"

I knew from his now relaxed manner, if not by the game he just played, that he was kidding.

"Well, I'm doing this report on what makes a ballplayer succeed..." but before I got too far, he said, "Joe, in order to succeed at baseball, first you have to love the game. I played baseball as far back as I can remember. I always wanted to be a major league baseball player and actually dreamed of playing while I was still in grammar school. But loving the game is not enough. You have to be willing to work hard at it and practice constantly."

"So," I asked, "desire and practice make you great?"

"It's not that simple. I wasn't really kidding about breaking my concentration. That's a big part of my success."

"What do you concentrate on?" I asked.

"I visualize the entire game before I play it. I think about everything that could possibly happen, every ball hit my way, and every pitch I might see. I see the ball being thrown by the pitcher in my mind's eye from the time it leaves his hand until the time it actually makes contact with my bat. By practicing this before the game, by rehearsing it mentally, I respond automatically in the game."

"Is that how you make it look so easy when you swing the bat?" I asked.

He just smiled and I knew the interview was over. I thanked Ted for his secrets and committed them to memory. Someday I'd have to account to Brother Colombo about why some succeed and others fail. Ted Williams' unique answer had given me a good start on my quest.

I wondered during that first season if I could also get Joe DiMaggio's secret of success. But perhaps because I spent a lot more time in the visitor's clubhouse, the right moment never quite presented itself. I would have given almost anything to get close to Joe, but it wasn't easy.

The closest I came to Joe in 1949 was during a terrible slump for the Yankee Clipper. It seemed as if he played games at a time without a hit. When he actually did connect, he wasn't hitting with his trademark authority.

One night, after Ralph and I returned home after Joe's third or fourth hitless day, Mom greeted us, "Hey, what's the matter with Joe Di?"

She was a Yankee fan and loved to follow Mel Allen's play by play.

"Just a slump, Ma," Ralph said. "He'll break out of it."

That wasn't good enough for Mom. She knew firsthand what it was to get a bit older and lose a step or two.

"Ralph," she said, "I'm gonna fix Joe Di one of my eggnogs. That'll turn things around for him. You wait and see if it doesn't get him some hits. Tell him tomorrow that you'll bring it on Saturday."

Ralph protested, but to no avail. When Mom's mind was made up, nothing could turn her back.

Mom was a great believer in eggnogs, her antidote for poor school grades, a lack of energy, and now, apparently, a low batting average.

On Saturday morning, Mom mixed a pint of fresh milk, added two raw eggs, and a generous amount of Hershey's chocolate syrup to make it palatable. As she poured it into a large glass jar, she instructed Ralph, "Make sure he drinks the whole thing. Pretend like I'm there watching."

Ralph had warned Joe that my mother was about to unleash her famous elixir upon him so that when Ralph and I entered the clubhouse that Saturday, Joe Di was actually on the lookout for us. Spotting Ralph, he quietly uttered, "Ralph, do you have your mother's eggnog for me?"

Joe Di took the paper bag with an air of nonchalance, but quickly scanned the clubhouse to make sure no one was looking. Ralph and I followed him as he slipped into the trainer's room where he carefully poured the entire contents of the chocolate eggnog from Mom's glass jar into his favorite beer mug. He then went back into the clubhouse where all the players were milling around, sat in his cubbyhole, and sipped the entire eggnog until the last ounce was finished.

I couldn't wait to see if Mom's eggnog would do the trick. For the Yankees' sake, I wanted Joe to start hitting again. But more than anything I wanted the Carrieri family, and particularly its youngest member, to occupy a special place in the heart of my idol.

Mom would have been nonplussed, but I almost jumped out of my visitor's uniform when Joe smashed a double down the left field line in his first at bat. I had to control myself. The visiting batboy wasn't supposed to show his emotions, but they were hard to control. When he hit a single in the fourth and another double in the sixth, I was thinking, "This is great."

By the end of the game, Joe was three for four, out of his slump, and the Yankees had won. His only out was a long drive to left center that traveled about 410 feet before Sam Mele of the Red Sox made a one-handed, leaping grab. Mom's eggnog had done the trick.

When I got to the Yankee clubhouse to meet Ralph, I wanted to yell out loud to anyone who could hear that my mom broke Joe out of his slump. But Ralph would've killed me for that one.

Right away, I made a point of walking past Joe's locker. I gave him my best "Hi Joe," and waited for sparks, fireworks, kudos, anything that would have translated into the recognition that Mom's eggnog so richly deserved. He gave me a big grin. From the little I had seen, that was a respectable amount of emotion from Joe Di.

As we got onto the subway an hour later, Ralph said, "Guess what I have in the bag?"

"Huh?"

Ralph took out a large photograph of Joe Di, which was autographed, "Thank you for your good wishes and the delicious drink. Sincerely, Joe DiMaggio."

"Don't you think Mom's gonna love it," he said.

"She'll frame it and put it in the living room," I answered.

"Joe doesn't say much, does he Ralph?"

"Joe's quiet. That's just his way. But a picture's worth a thousand words, Joe. You've heard that one, haven't you?"

"Yeah."

"Well, Joe said thanks, big time. And this picture will never let us forget it."

That wasn't a bad answer. I still hoped for a better one, though...one given to me in Joe's own words. That's what I was after, but that would wait for another day.

6

Quiet strength

On October 8, 1949 I was on the Yankee team bus on the way to Brooklyn. After two games in the Bronx, the subway Series between the Yankees and Dodgers was tied one game apiece. The first two games had been pitchers' duels, the winner each time scoring only one run.

I felt extraordinarily lucky to be traveling with the New York Yankees. They didn't need a visiting batboy in Brooklyn. But after the second game of the Series, Pete Sheehy gave me five dollars and told me to bring a bag of oranges to the Stadium for the next game – Sheehy's roundabout way of letting me know I could come along for the ride. The players relied on the oranges for a quick energy boost in the late innings.

The bus wound its way through the narrow streets of the Bronx toward the Third Avenue Bridge into Manhattan. We traveled south to the Brooklyn Bridge and crossed the bridge into the borough of Brooklyn. Stadium to stadium, it was probably all of twenty miles.

As I sat on the bus, I settled into a reverie, thinking back on the first two games at Yankee Stadium. Before the first game, I had again met Charlie DiGiovanna, the Dodgers' batboy. He didn't let me down, letting me take the field as the Dodgers' batboy when his team played in the Bronx.

In the first game, Allie Reynolds, the Yankee veteran and mainstay of the pitching staff, hurled a four-hit shutout. To everyone's surprise, Allie contributed two of the Bombers' four hits.

After the game, the Dodger clubhouse was like a morgue – cold, deathly still, the quiet cloud of gloom punctured only by the creak and frustrated slam of the lockers and the sound of cleats scraping the clubhouse floor.

As I did my chores, I noticed that Burt Shotton, the manager, called all his coaches into the manager's office and closed the door behind them.

"What's going on?" I asked Charlie.

"Damage control," he said. "Shotton won't take losing in stride. He'll have something to say to the guys about this one."

After twenty minutes, the office door was flung open. One of the managers motioned to George Natriano and whispered something in his ear. In a moment, George came up to me, put his hand on my shoulder and said quietly, "They want us out of here for a little bit, Joe."

Charlie DiGiovanna stayed behind.

I went back to the Yankee clubhouse to kill twenty minutes. The press was all over Allie Reynolds, light bulbs flashing, questions popping. He was an intelligent man who thought before he spoke. He nodded confidently and responded with straightforward answers to the reporters' questions.

"Been taking extra batting practice?" a reporter kidded him about his hit production.

"Just lucky, just lucky," said Allie. He seemed to mean it, but I had seen Allie Reynolds pitch all season long and I knew that luck had very little to do with it. In 1949, he won 17 games and lost only 6.

The bluff, bluster, and bombast of the Dodgers made better copy, but history is written by the winners...even the quiet, self-contained ones.

In 1949, Reynolds along with DiMaggio, Raschi, Henrich, Keller, and Lopat were among the senior members of the team. When any one of them spoke, the team listened. In a way that would seem surprising today, they set the tone for the '49 Yankees, which in its old-fashioned way demanded respect for elders and pride in the Yankee tradition.

Once during the past season, when Allie sat alone signing baseballs at one of the picnic tables in the center of the clubhouse, he said in a fatherly way, "How do you like your new job, Joe?"

"It's great," I answered.

"I notice you get here early, even on school days. How do you manage to do that?"

"I have a deal with my principal, Brother Colombo." I said. "He let's me leave school early on two conditions; I have to keep my grades up, and I'm supposed to prepare a report on why some players succeed where others fail."

"Brother Colombo is a wise man, Joe. He not only lets you have your boy's dream of being the batboy, he knows you can gain a lifetime's worth of experiences just by observing the players. He wants you to find the right role models for your life."

"I know and I appreciate it," Allie.

"If you want to know why a person succeeds, keep your eyes and ears open. Observe. Judge people more by what they do than what they say. And listen. Remember God gave us two ears and one mouth. Do you know why, Joe?" he asked me with a smile.

"Uh...not really," I answered.

"Because he wants us to listen twice as much as we speak."

I smiled but his words stayed with me.

When I returned in half an hour, nearly all the Dodgers had found their way to the team bus. Charlie was still hanging around though.

"Aren't you going back with the team?" I asked.

"My wife's picking me up," Charlie said.

"Your wife!"

"Yeah, Joe. How old do you think I am."

"I don't know, but not old enough to be married."

Charlie laughed. "I'm twenty-eight," he said as he poured himself a cup of coffee, lit an Old Gold cigarette, inhaled deeply, and leaned back against a locker.

"You know, Joe, I really consider myself a lucky guy. The Dodgers treat me like one of their own. The first time the Dodgers called a manager's meeting, I started to walk out. The manager told me to sit down; said where did I think I was going?"

Now I understood. Charlie always seemed like a lot more than the team's batboy. Some years later I wasn't surprised to find out that the Dodgers took Charlie to Los Angeles with them and bought him a house on the West Coast.

"What did Burt Shotton tell the Dodgers?" I asked, never expecting a reply.

"Look Joe, whatever I tell you will stay right in this room, okay?"

"You got my word on it," I swore.

"Well, it went like this. Shotton said 'Don't be intimidated by the Yankees. You guys fought hard for your pennant and man for man, you are every bit as good as any Yankee.' He said 'I don't care if the Yankees beat you, but...if you beat yourselves, there'll be a few less familiar faces on the team next year.' Then he went over each and every Yankee batter, talking about his strengths and weaknesses. The best part was probably when Preacher Roe asked Shotton what the book was on Yogi Berra."

"What happened then?" I asked.

"Shotton said, 'God only knows how to pitch to Yogi Berra.' Everyone laughed. But then Shotton said 'no, no, seriously. Yogi's a very dangerous hitter, mainly because he has no weaknesses. He can hit a pitch two feet over his head or two inches above the ground. I never saw anyone who could swing a bat so quickly and had such a strong pair of wrists.' Half kidding, Shotton finally said 'the only safe place to pitch him is right over the plate. He might miss it because it's the last place he'd expect a pitch.'"

I laughed at that story, wishing I could go back to the Yankee clubhouse and share it with Rizzuto, Berra, and the others. But I had to keep my word to Charlie.

"We'd better get going Joe," Charlie finally said. "You need a ride?"

"No thanks. I'm meeting my brother Ralph."

Less than twenty-four hours later I was back in the raucous, rowdy Dodger clubhouse. What a difference a day makes. In game two, Preacher Roe shut out the powerful Yankees, 1 to 0. Vic Raschi was the losing pitcher. It was a tough loss. He gave up just one run on seven hits.

When the game was over, the Dodgers came streaming through the clubhouse door, smiling, running, patting each other on the back, the sound of their cleats clicking briskly across the floor.

When things had settled a bit, the clubhouse was cleared out again as it had been the day before. I'm not sure why – perhaps it was because the Dodgers won – but this time I wasn't asked to go. I sat there quietly and listened as Shotton gathered everyone into the center of the room.

I guess he only threatened the team when they lost. Because when his Dodgers won, he was a preacher prophesying future glory as he whipped his Dodger congregation into a frenzy of false confidence.

"You can do it. You can beat the Yankees," he shouted.

"They're not supermen. They're human. Keep up the momentum. In a short series, we can beat these guys."

And one by one, Shotton talked about the weaknesses of the Yankees: DiMaggio, Collins, Lindell, Rizzuto, Woodling, Henrich, Johnson, Coleman, and Berra.

But try as he might, Shotton's efforts to diminish this galaxy of stars had a false ring, even to the thirteen-year-old batboy. In one sentence he'd describe the awesome attributes of a particular Yankee, and in the next sentence he'd tell his team that if they played to an impossible degree of perfection, this guy couldn't hurt them and there was no way they could lose.

Remembering Allie Reynolds words, I listened with two ears. After ten minutes, the team meeting was over. Despite the hype, I knew then that the Dodgers wouldn't outlast the Yankees in this World Series. Shotton knew it, and I sensed that now the Dodgers players, each and every one, knew it as well.

Someone on the bus shouted "There they are!"

I don't remember crossing the bridge into Brooklyn, but I received a rude awakening. First there was ten or twenty on each block. Pretty soon, there were hundreds. As we got closer to Ebbets Field, each succeeding block was more densely packed than the last with Dodgers' fans yelling at us, shaking their fists, holding their noses, waving both arms to tell us to go back where we belong. At first it was funny. But then the eggs and tomatoes started to pelt the bus.

We were escorted by two motorcycle cops in the front and a police cruiser in the rear. When the trip started, I thought they'd make for a grand entrance to Ebbets Field. Now I realized we just might need these guys.

According to plan, the bus drove through a center field gate. The hundreds of Dodgers fans that lined our path now became thousands. As soon as we entered Ebbets Field, we were roundly booed by 34,000 of the world's noisiest fans. Not taking any chances, the bus parked right next to the clubhouse. We went right in. Nobody asked for an autograph.

When the Dodgers arrived in the Bronx at about the same time for the first game of the series, Yankee Stadium's stands were nearly empty. The only sounds to greet the Dodgers were the snapping and flapping of banners and pennants won by the Yankee glory teams of years gone by. But here in Brooklyn, at eleven o'clock in the morning, the stands were nearly filled to capacity. Yankee Stadium held twice as many but they never made half the noise. To top it all, the Dodger Symphony made up of four or five musicians circulated through the stands, playing tunes to keep the spirits high.

The visitor's clubhouse at Ebbets Field was small, poorly lit and ventilated, and in a general state of disrepair. Instead of spacious wooden walk-in lockers like the visitors had in Yankee Stadium, each player had a metal locker with a wooden stool in front of it. The players dressed quickly and went outside for batting practice.

During the first two games at Yankee Stadium, the crowd roared whenever the Yankees got a hit or a Dodger made an out. At Ebbets Field, the roar was constant and it became noisier still whenever the Dodgers did something right.

In the ninth inning, the Yankees were down by a run, but the bases were loaded. Yogi Berra was on third, Bobby Brown on second, Gene Woodling on first.

A few years after this game, I heard a rookie named Bill Renna tell Woodling, "I'm going to take your job."

Woodling at 5'10" looked up at Renna, who was a huge man. With the ferocity of a pit bull, Woodling said, "You're not gonna take my job away until I'm ready to give it up."

Woodling wasn't boasting. He was as self-assured in 1949 as he was in 1953. He made the big plays time and again before a full house. Like so many of the Yankees of that era, he had the self-esteem and quiet confidence that comes from winning consistently and playing with the best.

Bill Renna was a little like the Dodgers on that October day in 1949. The "wannabes." But the Dodgers weren't ready to take it and the Yankees weren't giving it away.

"Observe. Judge people more by what they do than what they say." That's what Allie Reynolds had told me.

Cliff Mapes was in the on deck circle. I was watching the game from inside the dugout. I saw Casey Stengel say something to Johnny Mize, but I was out of earshot.

Casey Stengel. The Ol' Perfesser. The master of murdered diction, who rambled around every point he tried to make, who seemed disorganized and, at times, disoriented. But I watched what he did; there was no point in trying to understand what he said.

With the bases loaded, Casey pinch hit Johnny Mize, the "Big Cat," for Cliff Mapes. Cliff came back to the dugout. As Johnny searched for his bat, the crowd of 34,000 gave Mize a rousing welcome. Dodger fans knew him well from the many games he played at Ebbets Field as a visiting New York Giant. Mize was a recent addition to the Yankees, playing his twilight years with the Bronx Bombers.

The Yankee bench was breathlessly still. Casey's judgment was on the line.

Ralph Branca threw a fast ball to Mize and he jumped on it. The ball travelled deep, hitting the wire screen in right field. It was an enormous single that scored both Berra and Brown. The Bombers were ahead, the Yankee dugout was alive, and Stengel looked like a genius…and, for the first time all day, something finally had knocked the wind out of these Dodgers fanatics.

The "bums" never came back – in that one, or for the next two games.

I listened to and I observed the best. The Yankees. World Champions.

7

Transitions

After winning the 1949 World Series by a score of 10 to 6 in Game 5, the rollicking Yankees nearly blew the old roof off the visitor's clubhouse at Ebbets Field. The players were singing, shouting, laughing, and, with their arms hung around each other's necks, reliving every highlight of the big game. The dingy clubhouse was showered in light by the staccato "pops" of the photographer's flashes. The team emptied case after case of champagne, little of it actually drunk, most of it just popped and spritzed like a joyous display of emotional fireworks.

Back on the team bus, the partying never ended. Although everyone in a uniform was already damp, reeking of sticky, sweet champagne, there were two more cases of bubbly aboard for the trip back to the Bronx. There was also plenty of the team's favorite, Ballantine Beer and Ale, supplied by the Yankees' radio sponsor. There were even twelve-ounce Cokes for Yankee bat-boy Harry Jacobs, Ralph, and me.

As the team bus ground its gears and wound its way out of the despondent, devastated Borough of Brooklyn, there was no send-off from the mournful Dodger fans. They were taking it hard. It was almost as if they had disappeared, embarrassed as much by their outrageous cockiness as by their loss to the Yankees.

When the bus crossed the Willis Avenue Bridge into the Bronx, it was, as Yogi Berra would say, "deja vu all over again," except this time the streets were lined with throngs of cheering, adoring fans. Thousands upon thousands of Bronx residents were there to welcome the World Champion Yankees. We were floating on air. Better than anything I had ever known or experienced, I was intoxicated by the adulation of strangers, by this thing called "fame."

As we neared the Stadium, the bus inched its way through the surging crowd. Outside the Stadium gate, dozens of New York City cops were waiting for us. They escorted the players one at a time into the clubhouse. Once inside, reporters and photographers had their notebooks and cameras ready. There were more interviews, more photo sessions. The players, who were expected to pack their equipment for spring training six months down the road, dragged their feet and basked in the glow, savoring the fine wine of this moment as long as possible.

Ralph and I picked up old uniforms, shined shoes, and helped the players pack their bags. By the time we were done, it was almost ten o'clock, and only Big Pete, Little Pete, Ralph, Harry Jacobs, and I were left. Or so I thought. We were carrying equipment to the trainer's room when we startled Joe DiMaggio, who was lying face down on the trainer's table. He seemed a little embarrassed. He sat up slowly, a towel draped across his midsection. His body seemed one big ache, his face pale, and his torso and legs a patchwork of black and blue. Joe Di, who had just come back from a bout of pneumonia, played the Series on courage alone, as if his spirit had taken command of his aching muscles and joints, and his exhausted body.

"Get me a beer Pete," Joe asked.

Sheehy went into the trainer's room and quickly reappeared with a Ballantine and a large beer cup. Joe Di tilted the cup, poured the beer slowly and deliberately, emptying the bottle to the last drop.

He looked at us and said, "I'm getting too old for this."

He took a few sips and then headed for a long hot shower. He was still there twenty minutes later when we had just about finished the last of our chores.

You couldn't help but feel for him. He must've been going through a lot of self-doubt. He didn't have an impressive World Series. Aside from some timely hitting by "Old Reliable," Tommy Henrich, and Johnny Mize, this had been a pitchers' Series. Allie Reynolds, Vic Raschi, and Joe Page shared the spotlight.

But the fans still worshiped Joe Di. They always would. But he knew he was approaching that time when he would be but a fond memory. It must have been particularly hard for him at age thirty-four to face a future where he was just Mr. DiMaggio, neither the heart and soul of the World Champion Yankees nor the toast of New York. Pretty soon he'd have to let go. At age thirteen, for my sake, I just hoped he'd hold on a little bit longer.

Harry, Ralph, and I followed Joe Di out of the clubhouse. It was after ten o'clock. Only Sheehy stayed behind. Harry lived in a tenement on Willis Avenue and 138th Street; ours was just a couple of blocks further. When we walked through the door, the celebration continued. Mom and Dad, beaming with pride, were waiting up for Ralph and me with sandwiches and cold milk. Mom loved to find out who said what to whom and where everyone was going for the winter. The one question she didn't ask, and the one I couldn't let go of, was whether Joe DiMaggio would return the following spring to the Bronx.

During the next few weeks, a foreign invasion of New York City wouldn't have gotten as much news coverage as Joe Di's prospective retirement. Every possible slant on the story was covered by the City's sports pages. The majority of sportswriters clearly believed that Joe couldn't or wouldn't reappear at Yankee Stadium the following year. It depressed me to even think about it, but I was so obsessed with Joe Di's departure that I could think of nothing else. I read every article, picking up two or three newspapers at a corner newsstand on the way to school and another couple on my way home. During that time, I'm sure I read every edition of the New York Times, Daily News, Daily Mirror, Herald Tribune, New York World–Telegram, and New York Post.

Aside from my feelings as a team member, as a Yankee fan I knew that Joe's Di's presence on the team couldn't be measured by his fielding or his batting average, hits, or runs batted in. The sum was far greater than any of those parts. Although he said little, Joe had a mystique that filled a room and brought a crowded stadium alive. Frank Shea, the Yankee pitcher, probably summed it up best when he said that if Joe Di were playing, he knew he would win. His very presence in the lineup changed the balance of power between the Yankees and their opponents. But even more importantly, Joe had a way of demanding and getting the best from those that shared the field with him.

Late in October, Ralph found me scanning the sports pages again. "All you do lately is read the sports pages. The World Series is over. What're you reading about?"

"It's the great debate," I said.

"Is Joe Di or isn't Joe Di coming back. I really hope he doesn't quit now…not before I get to talk to him about the meaning of success. He's the most important person I'm ever going to talk to."

With a big smile on his face, Ralph asked, "Do you really want to know for sure whether he'll be back?"

"More than anything," I said.

"Well, there's one way to find out without waiting for spring training."

"What's that?"

"Let's go to Yankee Stadium."

"You mean Pete Sheehy will know?" I asked.

"Of course. Pete knows everything about the Yankees – past, present, and future."

I jumped up from the couch. On a chilly Saturday morning in late October, we donned our Yankee hats, put on our winter jackets, and walked briskly to the ballpark.

Less than a month after the excitement of the World Series, the neighborhood around River Avenue and 161st Street was all but deserted.

"How do you know Pete'll be there?" I asked.

"I just know. Pete's always there."

We knocked on the front door of the administrative offices. Joe Serrano looked through the glass and let us in.

"Come to visit with Pete?" he said.

"Yeah. How'd you know?" Ralph asked.

"Because he's the only one here besides me and some maintenance men."

Ralph and I hurried down the stairs and through the maze underneath the Stadium. The clubhouse door was unlocked. We went in and there was Pete sitting in the center of the room taking inventory.

"You know Pete," I started, "I've been reading twenty articles that say Joe Di's. . . .

"Don't worry Joe," Pete cut me off.

"DiMaggio's coming back for at least one more year, just like I told Ralph on the last day of the Series."

I turned to Ralph who had the biggest, broadest grin on his face. He had a good laugh on me, knowing all the while that Joe Di was coming back.

"Why don't you guys have a seat. Time for me to take a break anyway.

"I told Ralph that I knew Joe Di was coming back when I was helping him pack. Without thinking about it, I started to pack Joe's spikes and gloves with his personal effects. He looked at me and said 'Pete, put the spikes and gloves in the bench locker.' I looked at him in shock. He smiled and said, 'That's right. I'm coming back.'"

Pete gave me a wink, and said, "Let me go get a beer. I have something to tell you two."

Pete came back with a Ballantine and two Cokes. After a long draw on his beer, Pete looked at Ralph and said, "You've got a choice, Ralph."

Ralph responded with a surprised "Huh."

"I just got a call from Harry Jacobs. He joined the Navy – so he won't be coming back as the batboy next season. But that isn't all. Last week George Natriano came in and said he's not feeling all that well. He's getting up there, you know. I expect he'll be heading down to Florida. So we're going to need someone to be the new clubhouse man as well. You have a choice, Ralph. You can either be the Yankee batboy or the visiting clubhouse man. You don't have to tell me now, but I'd like to know in the next couple weeks or so."

The significance of what Pete had just said hit me like a bolt of lightning. I was no longer going to be the visiting batboy. I knew the progression at Yankee Stadium. No matter what Ralph chose to do, I was going to move up the clubhouse ladder. Wow!

Ralph was stunned and didn't give his answer. Pete reassured him, saying, "Ralph, you don't have to give me an answer now. Think it over. Call me in a week or so... or, even better, come and visit me."

As we got ready to go, Pete said, "Let me know as soon as you can Ralph. Either way, you'll come out ahead. But it's your choice."

During the next couple of weeks, Ralph was unusually quiet. He was at a crossroads in his life. He graduated from Cardinal Hayes High School the previous June, and was now facing decisions about his future and his career. Ralph was a good student. He had achieved a fair measure of success by attending Cardinal Hayes – no small feat for a working class Italian kid in the 1940s.

Ralph loved being on the field with the Yankees, playing ball, dressing in pinstripes. During batting practice, he liked nothing better than playing the outfield between DiMaggio and Keller, pitching to Yogi Berra, or laughing at the player's jokes like the insider he was. When he had graduated from Cardinal Hayes the previous June, George Stirnweiss, the second baseman, gathered all the players in the clubhouse to congratulate Ralph. Stirnweiss presented Ralph with a silver pen and pencil set and $50 – tokens of the team's appreciation and respect for

Ralph.

Now he had the opportunity to step into the Yankee batboy's shoes, a job that would have been a dream come true for any boy in America.

But Ralph wasn't a kid anymore. My big brother was now a man who had to make his own decisions.

After a week of agonizing over his choice, Ralph woke me up early the following Saturday morning. Rubbing my eyes, I looked out at pitch darkness. I peered at the clock.

"Ralph, it's only five o'clock."

"I know he said. We're going to the Stadium."

"Are you crazy?"

"No. I gotta talk to Pete and he's an early riser."

Too tired to argue, I reluctantly dressed, ate a bowl of cold cereal, and walked to Yankee Stadium with Ralph. We got there before seven o'clock but it was shut tight. We walked to the nearest corner, found a telephone booth, and called Pete. When he hung up, Ralph told me that Sheehy answered on the second ring and wasn't surprised to hear Ralph's voice.

"He told us to come by the front door and he'll open it for us."

I followed groggily along.

Pete didn't say a word as we followed him through the underground passageways into the clubhouse. This mystery man was dressed as he always was – black oxfords, no socks, white tee-shirt, and chinos. He offered us coffee, which was already brewed. He looked like he had been up a while.

Although Pete was rumored to have an apartment on 86th Street in Manhattan, he rarely left Yankee Stadium on season or off. He slept there and he ate there. He had no family but the

Yankees. He had no home but Yankee Stadium. Pete was never married and he never mentioned his relations. He lived for the New York Yankees and although he never was the center of attention, he was always close to it. In his time, he shared in the glory of Ruth, Gehrig, DiMaggio and Mantle, and, oddly enough, outlasted all of them.

"So what is it Ralph? You've made your decision."

Ralph said, "I really haven't made up my mind and I'd like to hear what you have to say first."

"Well, it's your decision. I can think out loud, which might help.

"You're eighteen. You're out of school. You gotta think about your future. You can only be the batboy for another two or three years tops. On the other hand, the clubhouse job opens up every ten or twenty years. It gives you some steady income, more like a real job than being batboy. If I was in your shoes, I'd say to myself that I could be around baseball a while longer, maybe even support a family, if I took the clubhouse job."

"I was leaning toward that decision," Ralph said.

"I think you made the right choice."

"And Joe," said Pete, "I guess you've already figured out that you're moving up. We hired an older kid to be batboy, so you're going to be the new ballboy."

I smiled from ear to ear.

"Come visit me, Ralph, before spring. It's gets lonely during the winter and I like your company. Bring Joe along if you can tear him away from the books."

I gave Pete a quizzical look, wondering how he knew about my pounding the books in the off-season.

"I've been talking with Brother Colombo and he wants to

make sure that you're on the right road, that is, mixing baseball and school in the proper combination."

I was shocked that Pete had been talking with my principal.

"What did Brother Colombo have to say?" I asked.

"Well, that's between me and Brother Colombo," Pete answered. "But you got nothing to worry about."

"Nothing to worry about," I said to myself. To me that could only mean that there was something to worry about. I couldn't wait to get to school on Monday morning to investigate this conversation from the other end.

During the walk home, Ralph seemed relieved but less than overjoyed.

"You sorry you didn't take the batboy job, Ralph?" I asked.

He seemed surprised by the question.

"No. I'm not sorry."

"You don't look too happy."

"You wouldn't understand, Joe. Hey, anyway, it's great you moved up a notch. You'll like being in the clubhouse with the Yankees. I'm going to miss being with the guys."

"Is that it?" I asked.

"No. I'll do okay in the visitor's clubhouse. I mean, I'll still be seeing everyone."

"How long was George in the visitor's clubhouse?" I asked.

"Forever, I think. But I won't be there forever, Joe. It's good for a while, but it won't last. I think I'm a little like Joe Di. Couple years. That's it. Only Pete Sheehy goes on and on."

We both laughed.

"This is a great place to be. But it's not my future," said Ralph. "I guess I'm just getting used to that fact."

I looked at big brother. It was a little too much for me to

understand. I was going to be the Yankee ballboy. As far as I was concerned, it only got better and better. I planned to stay with the Yankees forever.

8

Brother Colombo

For two days after becoming the Yankee ballboy, I was sitting on top of the world – almost. Since the Yankee batboy was king, I had a little way to go. But as the ballboy, I was the heir apparent – a prince with great expectations. My elation, however, was tinged with a bit of anxiety. I really didn't know why Brother Colombo had been talking with Pete Sheehy and I had to find out. With things going so well for me, I couldn't take a chance that something could go wrong.

The Monday following the conversation with Sheehy, I was up early. I had been anxious and had had trouble sleeping. I knew Brother Colombo was in his office long before he greeted his charges on the school steps at 8:40. Although I usually left home at 8:30, I was out of the house before eight o'clock.

During the five minute walk to school, I rehearsed my lines. I really couldn't come right out and say "Hey Brother, I hear you've been talking about me with Pete Sheehy." That would be crossing the line that separated principal from pupil. Brother Colombo didn't owe me an answer. Instead, I had to be artful, humbly gathering the necessary information without treading on my principal's prerogatives. This wasn't easy, but I had gotten a lot of practice over the years.

"Good morning Brother!" I imagined myself saying.

"You're here quite early, Joseph," was Brother Colombo's imagined reply.

"I got up early to make the 7:30 Mass."

Forget it. That one would never fly. He knew me too well. I never got up early to go to Mass, except on Sunday, and he just might check out my story. Better try another tack.

"Hey Brother. Good to see you. Guess what. I just found out I've been promoted to Yankee ballboy."

"That's great Joe."

"Yeah, Brother. Pete Sheehy just told me last Saturday. You know Pete don't you Brother?"

That was good if Brother took the bait. If he simply said, "As a matter of fact, I've never met Pete Sheehy," then I'd have to try another line – like....

"Yeah. Pete's my boss at Yankee Stadium. He's been real good to me. He made sure I got on the team bus when the World Series went to Brooklyn. He's always asking me about how I'm doing in school. By the way, Brother, everything's okay at school, isn't it."

St. Jerome's Boys Grammar School and its complement, St. Jerome's Girls, were the educational hub of a sprawling Irish neighborhood in the South Bronx. (The boys and girls were separated after third grade for what were, in those days, obvious reasons.) Although some Italian families had made their way into the neighborhood by the 1940s, they were few and far between. In fact, when I came to St. Jerome's in the first grade, I was one of the first Italian kids in the school. My earliest memories there include a fair, freckled Irish youngster named Michael Byrd, who approached me and said, "Show me your knife?"

"Knife?" was my startled reply. "I don't have a knife."

"Don't lie to me," Michael said.

"Why would I have a knife?" I asked.

"Because you are Italian."

Being fairly logical even at this tender age, I said, "If you're saying all Italians carry knives, you're casting stones at the Holy Father. Don't you know the Pope is Italian?"

"We don't believe in that Pope," said Michael.

Years later, I was delighted to find out that Michael had become a priest – who, I imagine, had finally found a pope, whether Italian or Polish, whom he could believe in.

Brother Colombo was St. Jerome's benign, but omnipotent, ruler. Colombo was his first name; I never learned his last. The title "Brother" came from his membership in the Christian Brothers, a religious order that required vows of chastity, poverty, and obedience from its members. The discipline imposed by those vows carried over. Brother Colombo ran a tight ship.

At times, it seemed as if there were two Brother Colombo's. One came to my homeroom once a month to hand out report cards. There, this stocky, determined man with steely blue eyes that went right through you stood in front of the whole class. He'd call up each one of us as he quickly reviewed the latest results. Depending on what he saw in the report card, he offered his congratulations for a fine job, lent encouragement for an improved performance, or, with a pained look on his face, he uttered those infamous words: WHEN WILL YOU LIVE UP TO YOUR GOD-GIVEN POTENTIAL? Nearly everyone I knew at St. Jerome's had heard those words at some point in his academic career.

This approach was generally effective, if not quite modern,

but Brother Colombo exhibited no self-doubts about the role he was supposed to play in molding young lives. He demanded respect and it was never in short supply around him.

Brother Colombo was a different man outside school, though. He was friendly, warm, and caring. During May and June, he'd often organize field trips on Saturdays to Randall's Island in the East River, where there were (and still are) about twenty-five baseball fields. As we split into teams, Brother was the steady pitcher and he did a pretty respectable job.

On one of these trips, Brother must have noticed that one of the boys, Richie Pryor, was always borrowing a glove from someone on the other team. Sometimes Richie got stuck with a lefty glove, which was hard for him to use since he was a righty. At other times, Richie just played the outfield without any glove at all. We knew Richie's mom, who was single, couldn't afford to buy him a glove. I had Ralph's glove, which I was very proud to use – but who wouldn't have been, the glove had belonged to Phil Rizzuto.

On the hike home, I overheard Brother Colombo ask Richie whether his mother could afford to buy him a baseball glove. Richie just shook his head. That was it. No more questions.

A week later, Brother Colombo was joined again by the merry band of Bobby Corbo, Bobby Woods, Richie Pryor, Michael Byrd, Hippo Haggerty, Ed Tierney, Michael Noonan, Michael O'Neil, Denis Dillon, Mike Flynn and me. As soon as we got to Randall's Island, Brother tossed a brown bag to Richie. His face lit up like a Christmas tree as he took out an off-the-shelf, auto-graphed, Charlie Keller glove by Rawlings. The new leather smelled as fresh as it looked.

Brother Colombo once said that he lived on $15 a week.

That's what a Brother was paid – not really pay, just spending money. Even in 1949, that wasn't much to get around on. Brother blew a week's pay to put a smile on a kid's face. An extraordinary act of kindness. I'll never forget it.

I knocked on Brother Colombo's door. He motioned me in. He gave me a stern, serious look.

"Yes, Joe. How can I help you?"

I was tongue-tied and couldn't get anything out.

"Mr. Sheehy told me that you had called him."

O God. I blew it.

"Is there anything wrong with that?"

"No, Brother, but...I was just a...curious...." He had me right where he wanted me – way out in front of the pitch. All my rehearsal for nothing.

"Don't worry. You're doing fine, Joe. I've been speaking to all your teachers. You're not only keeping your grades up, you're doing better in every class and every subject and your overall average is up five points."

"That's good news Brother."

"You know Joe, I took a chance in allowing you to leave school early without the permission of the Board of Education. In fact, let me tell you a secret. I did call the Board and I asked them for permission to allow you to leave school at noon so that you could go to Yankee Stadium for the home games. They turned me down."

My heart sank. I thought Brother was setting me up for a big letdown.

"But I have confidence in you, Joe. So, in spite of what the Board has said, I'm going to bend the rules. You can continue to go provided you keep up your end of the deal."

"I won't let you down, Brother," I said, breathing a little easier.

"Don't let yourself down, Joe.

"Now that you have a year's experience under your belt, tell me something about what makes great ballplayers succeed."

"Oh boy. Well. . . . "

"I told you a year ago that that's part of your assignment. Now that you've had a year to think about it, and one full baseball season with the World Champion Yankees, I want you to start to formulate an answer."

"Well, Brother, I noticed that the great players are in really good shape. Even Joe DiMaggio, who's older than most of the other players, is in great physical condition. Ted Williams as well."

"Why do you think they're in great shape?"

"So they can play their best game."

"What else have you learned?" asked Brother.

"Well, they have confidence. Not the loud kind like the Dodgers. But they know they're good and they know they can win."

"Do you think that their confidence comes from achieving goals, Joe?"

"I guess you could say that you have to have goals to succeed, Brother."

"That's good, Joe. Now tell me why you said that."

"Well, I can think of a funny story I heard after a game. One day in the clubhouse the players were talking about success. Bobby Brown said that you have to have a goal in order to succeed. 'Without a goal, there's too much flip-flopping, indecision, and no direction to your life,' he said. If you don't have a goal, then you won't work towards that end. If you want to be a major league baseball player, but don't set that firmly in your mind as a goal, then you won't take the necessary steps to reach that goal. But if being a major league ballplayer is your goal, then you'll do everything you have to do in order to reach that goal.'"

"That's good, Joe. You've learned a lot."

"There's more, Brother. After Bobby Brown had made that speech, Yogi Berra said 'Bobby, I had no goal to be a major league baseball player and here I am. How do you figure that.'"

"Bobby smiled and said 'Yogi, in your case, there may not be an answer, but I think there is. I think your goal was to be a baseball player, only it was subconscious. Because, since you were a kid, you played baseball every chance you had.' Yogi just nodded.

"Then Bobby Brown said 'I already achieved my first lifetime goal, which was to become a major league baseball player. Now my goal is to become a doctor. I felt there was a conflict in having two goals at the same time so I concentrated all my efforts toward becoming a ballplayer. Now that I have achieved that goal, I have concentrated all my efforts to study every night past midnight until I become a medical doctor.'"

"Doc Brown is a pretty amazing person, isn't he Joe?"

"He sure is. I've never heard of a baseball player studying to become a doctor."

"Joe, you're fortunate to be with people who want to want to be their best, who want to succeed.

"By the way, Joe, what's your goal?"

"Well, I started as the visiting batboy. The next step is ballboy. That's the progression at Yankee Stadium, and I just found out the other day that I will be the ballboy next season. But my real goal is to become the Yankee batboy."

"That's good. Do you have any other goals?"

"Yeah Brother. I'd like to get to know Joe DiMaggio. I'd like to be able to talk to him. I'd like to find out what makes him a great ballplayer?"

"Did you try this past season to talk to him?"

"A couple of times. But it's very hard to get close to Joe. He doesn't say much and he keeps to himself. I'm afraid if I get him at a bad moment, he might tell me to take a hike. Still in all, it's great just to be in the same room with him. There's really something special about him. I don't know how to define it."

"And you think Joe may be able to define it for you."

"That's my assignment, Brother."

"Right Joe. I'm sure when you do talk with him, he'll give you an answer worth remembering."

"I think he will. Maybe next year I'll get to know him better. I'll be in the Yankee clubhouse all season long. That can't hurt."

"Good Joe. Keep trying. If you learn something, then I'll have achieved one of my goals."

"Okay, Brother. I'll keep you posted."

"Do that. Now get going. We've got work to do."

9

Persistence, talent, and the power of love

The Yankees picked up in 1950 where they had left off in 1949 – playing the Brooklyn Dodgers. On a chilly afternoon in early April, Yankee Stadium filled for the cross-town rematch between the World Champion Yankees and the up-and-coming Dodgers. Although the Yankees had beaten the "bums" in the World Series not six months before, the Dodgers were undaunted.

This was an exhibition game and would never factor in either team's won/lost column, but you'd never know it by the noise level in the Stadium. The raucous, rowdy Dodger fans had invaded the Bronx in force. As any New Yorker from the '40s and '50s could tell you, Dodger fans were a special breed – not just fans, but "fanatics" with a frenzied dedication to their team.

And the team thrived on their support. They were the new kids on the block – proud, cocky upstarts who wanted everyone to know that they had arrived.

The Dodgers also knew the Yankees were the team to beat. Coming off their defeat in the 1949 World Series, the Dodgers wanted to show that they could conquer baseball's best team. Not only were the Yankees World Champions, they were everyone's favorite to repeat in 1950.

It was great to be back at Yankee Stadium. The cold weather couldn't dampen the air of excitement that was always part of a new season. I was especially looking forward to catching up with Charlie DiGiovanna, the Dodgers' batboy.

"Hey, Joe the ballboy," Charlie called to me as I shagged balls in the outfield before the game, "You're moving up in the world."

"Yeah. How do I look in pinstripes?"

"It's you."

"You going to be around later?" I asked.

"Yeah. Stop by the visitor's clubhouse."

"I'll see you after the game," I hollered.

Since this was my first day as the ballboy, I felt I was under a microscope magnified 50,000 times. The ballboy had a high profile. He was on the field all the time and had to be alert. Any miscue, like a bobbled ball, might be greeted with a Bronx cheer. I didn't need that my first day on the job.

Unlike the batboy, who got a break when his team took the field, the ballboy was always on the move and had to cover a lot of territory. He retrieved every foul ball, catching it off the screen behind home plate, chasing it down the base line, or getting the relay from the umpire at first or third. In modern times, there's a ballboy or ballgirl along both the first and third base lines. In days of yore, one boy did it all.

Each game started with seventy-two balls. The umpire put six of these in his over-sized pockets. I kept the rest by me. I also kept mental notes on the umpire's supply. God help the ballboy if the game stopped because an inattentive ballboy let an umpire run out of balls.

Sitting on the edge of a stool, positioned to the left of the Yankee dugout along the first base line, I was tense, but ready. At two o'clock, the umpire called "Play ball," and seconds later the first foul ball went screaming behind home plate onto the screen. My terrified heart pumped frantically. I jumped off my stool, raced under the screen and waited...while the ball rolled slowly off and plopped into my hands. I put it in my pocket and ran back to my station. Although it seemed like an eternity, my rite of passage took all of ten seconds.

A couple of times when the Dodgers were up, I chased some foul balls near the Dodgers' dugout. As I ran over to field the ball, Charlie would run out of the dugout, pick it up and underhand it to me. When this happened in the ninth inning, Charlie yelled, "Joe, after the game, don't forget to come by. I'll buy you a Coke."

"I'll see you there."

After the game, which the Dodgers won, I hurried my shower in the Yankee clubhouse, quickly put on my street clothes, and rushed to the visitor's clubhouse. I was worried that I'd be locked out. When I got there, I thought I was out of luck. There were about twenty reporters and photographers milling outside the door. Before the press was allowed in the locker room, they gave the team a chance to have meeting or just settle down. Fred the doorman spotted me and moved through the crowd. He put his hand on my should and said, "Come on in, Joe."

"Is it okay? No meeting going on?"

"No meeting today. Besides, your brother Ralph's in charge. He said you can go on in."

I felt ten feet tall. As I walked past some of the best known sportswriters in New York, I could feel their stares on my back, wondering how come this fourteen-year-old kid was walking right past them into the visitor's clubhouse.

My brother Ralph spotted me.

"Hey Joe," he said, "you made some friends. Charlie's looking for you."

The Dodgers had already showered and dressed. I went over, shook hands with Charlie, and then gave him a big hug.

"I hope you had a good winter," Charlie said.

"It was. I studied hard, but the best part was just thinking about coming back here and starting all over again."

"Same with me, Joe, except for that part about studying all winter. I live for baseball. I don't know what I'd do without it. So you're hitting the books."

"I have to hit the books, Charlie. It's part of my deal with Brother Colombo, my principal at St. Jerome's. That's how I get out of school early to come to these ball games. I can't let my marks fall off. I'm supposed to prepare a report on what makes a ballplayer successful."

"Sounds like an interesting assignment," Charlie said. "Who have you talked to so far?"

"Just a few people. But some good ones, like Ted Williams. I want to talk to Joe DiMaggio but the timing is never right."

"So you're not just interested in talking to Yankees?"

"That's right," I said.

"So you just might like to speak to a few of the Dodgers?"

"I was hoping you'd say that, Charlie."

"I've never given that particular question a great deal of thought myself," said Charlie, "but let me call some of the guys over. Jackie, Duke, Ralph Branca. Could you guys come over here for a few?"

I shook my head in amazement. Here was the Dodgers' batboy calling over some of baseball's greatest players. Without hesitation, they all came. There was no doubt about how much the

Dodgers loved and respected Charlie DiGiovanna.

"You remember Joe," Charlie began, "the visiting batboy from last year."

"Hey Joe," they all said, shaking my hand and patting me on the back.

"You're not telling the Yankees our secrets, are you Joe?" Duke Snider kidded me.

"Hey. I can keep a confidence."

"Guys, Joe has something to ask you and it's real serious. So don't fool around."

I was on the spot, too embarrassed to say, "Hey, what makes you guys great?"

Charlie, ever sensitive to how other people were taking things, noticed I was hesitating. Right away, he picked up the ball.

"Guys, Joe has a project given to him by his grammar school principal, and it's one of the conditions that he was allowed to cut class and come to Yankee Stadium during school time."

"What's the project?" Jackie asked.

"I have to find out what makes a person great...well, more particularly, what makes a baseball player succeed. Or to put it another way, what makes one player succeed and another player not succeed...even though they have the same natural abilities."

"You know, Joe," Jackie said, "I've often thought of that question. I can't answer it for anyone else, but for me the answer can be summed up in a word. Persistence."

Jackie then hesitated for a moment and seemed to be lost in deep thought.

"No Joe. Let me change that answer. There are a number of

reasons why a person succeeds in life or in baseball. It's just that in my case, the biggest reason is persistence."

"Are there any other reasons, Jackie?"

"Well, number one, you have to love the game. You have to love what you are doing. This way, it's not a job or a chore, it's a pleasure. And as I'm sure you know, Joe, when you're doing what you like to do, you're going to do it well.

"When I was a kid I would play ball everyday, no matter if it was cold or rainy. I would rather play baseball then eat when I was a kid and, quite frankly, I still feel the same way."

"Anything else, Jackie?" I asked.

"In the beginning, I played baseball because I loved the game. And while I've always loved it, it became clear to me that I had a goal...no, not a goal...a mission. A mission to be the first Negro player in the major leagues. I took a lot of abuse. When I was first traveling with the team, I couldn't stay at the same hotel as my teammates. It would've been easy for me to quit or just go to the Negro Leagues. But I felt my mission was to make it easier for every other Negro player in the future. So I stuck it out. And that, Joe, is the secret of my success. I never gave up. I refused to quit."

By this time, some of the younger Dodgers had gathered round, listening attentively to Jackie hold forth on his theory of success.

Charlie turned to Ralph Branca, a Dodgers' pitcher.

"How would you answer Joe's question, Ralph?"

"In my case, Joe, I would say the most important reason I succeeded is my God-given physical abilities. I'm 6'2", 200 pounds. I have a great deal of stamina and I can throw a fast ball ninety miles an hour. I'm not bragging. I just want to make the point that without my natural talents, I don't think I ever could have become a major league baseball player."

Just as Ralph Branca finished, a dozen reporters and photographers were ushered in and virtually stole the players from me. I was really hoping to get Duke Snider's ideas on success but, it seemed, that would have to wait for another day.

Charlie must've sensed my disappointment.

"Let's see if we can't find someone else to talk to, Joe."

I followed Charlie to the far end of the clubhouse where Roy Campanella had yet to be discovered by the reporters.

"Roy," Charlie began, "I'm helping Joe out. He's trying to get a report together on what makes baseball players tick."

Roy began to laugh.

"If you find that one out, Joe, let me know. Sometimes you feel strong and you get up there, strike out, and go 0 for 5. The next game, you duck a pitch, the ball hits your bat, and you're on base with a double. You just can't figure this game out."

"That's not really the kind of answer I was looking for," I said. What I really want to know is what made you succeed in baseball where another player with your talents might have failed?"

"I can answer that very easily. I know what makes other people fail, which is, that they don't take the game seriously enough. By that I mean that they have too many other things going for them. In order to succeed, you have to be single-minded. You must focus on what you want, and then you must specialize in the field that you're best at."

We were interrupted by a reporter who had finally caught up to Roy. Figuring that this was my cue to leave, I thanked Roy, said good-bye to Charlie and headed for the clubhouse door. I was almost out the door, when someone called me from behind.

"Son, come back here for a moment." It was Roy.

When I walked backed to him, he told me to sit down. He must've gotten rid of the sportswriter, because there was no else around but Roy and me.

"You know…" he said, "I'm going to tell you something that may have nothing to do with baseball, but I think it has everything to do with baseball. And with life," he added.

"You can't be good at baseball or anything else for that matter, unless you have love. You can't have hatred in your heart, be angry, and hostile, and still perform well. That is why before every game, I say a little prayer. I don't pray that the other team won't do well, but I pray that I will do well and live up to my God-given capabilities."

"The power of love, Roy?"

"To me, Joe, that's what success is all about."

"Thanks Roy."

After I left Roy, I sought out Charlie. I wanted to wish him and the Dodgers well before I left. I didn't know if I'd be seeing them come October.

"I got some good answers today, Charlie. Thanks."

"Glad I could help. I won't say good-bye, just I'll be seeing you. It'll be World Series time before we know it."

"You gotta think positive, Charlie."

"I always do."

10

Mississippi Mud and other tricks of the trade

Just before game time, the umpires would gather in their room in the back of the clubhouse for a pregame ritual – rubbing up the game balls. As I waited just inside the doorway to their room, my canvas ball bag in hand, one of the umpires would unwrap six dozen new baseballs while another dipped his hands into a Maxwell House coffee can. When he lifted his hands out, they were coated with a black mud that he rubbed on each shiny ball until the last one was a dull brown.

Legend had it that this mud originated on the banks of the Mighty Mississippi. The so-called Mississippi Mud was transported from the river's edge to waiting umpires across the land.

When the umpire finished rubbing up the game balls, I'd pick them up, throw them in my bag, and head for my station along the first base line.

It was my job to make sure that the home plate umpire never ran low on balls. Six dozen were usually enough to see him through nine innings. But, occasionally, because a lot of balls were fouled into the stands or, maybe because the game went into extra innings, seventy-two balls were long gone before the final out was made. When that happened, I'd run into the Yankee clubhouse, open a baseball twelve-pack or two and, and without ever leaving my Bronx backyard,take a dip in the

Mississippi.

Early in the 1950 season, with the Yankees leading 5 to 3 under the lights, we had gone through sixty plus balls by the sixth inning. At the end of the inning, I ran to the clubhouse to rub up the balls for the first time. I had hardly slipped into the dugout on my way to the clubhouse when I heard a familiar voice say, "Make 'em nice and dark, Joe."

"Huh," was my startled reply. I turned around.

"Nice and dark Joe."

I was looking right at Frank Crosetti, the third base coach, who was speaking without ever looking in my direction. His eyes never left the playing field. Like a ventriloquist, his lips hardly moving, he said, "Make 'em dark, Joe."

"Okay, Frank, whatever you say."

So, just as Frank Crosetti had ordered, I rubbed up the balls as dark as the Mississippi Mud would allow, tossed them in my canvas bag, and went back on the field. By the bottom of the seventh inning, I was supplying the dark balls to Bill Sommers, the home plate umpire. Both pitchers made a strong showing down the stretch. No more runs were scored and the Yankees held on to win.

Back in the clubhouse after the game, I bumped into Frank coming out of the coaches' room. With a big smile on his face, he said, "You did good tonight, Joe."

"What did I do?"

"You know why the umps put that mud on the ball, don't you?"

"Takes the shine off?"

"Right. Gives the pitchers and fielders a better throwing grip."

"Well, what difference does it make whether I make them

light or dark before handing them to the ump?" I asked.

"Because we're playing under the lights."

"I don't get it," I said.

"After it's dark, with the lights on, it's hard for the hitters to see the ball. So you want to make the ball as white as possible so they can see it better."

"Okay. But how come you wanted me to rub them dark tonight?"

"Because we were up by two runs. The other team couldn't see the dark balls. And even though our guys couldn't see them either, well…we don't care 'cause we're up by two runs and all we gotta do is hold the lead for a couple innings. And Joe… besides the umpires…you're the only one who can touch the balls. If I or the other coaches went near 'em, the other team would probably try and stop the game."

"I get it. So that's why you didn't want anyone to see you talking to me.

"Right."

"And I guess if the Yankees were behind in the score, you'd hardly want any mud on the ball at all."

"You learn quick, Joe."

Jim Turner, the pitching coach, who heard the whole conversation said, "Where do you get that stuff, Frank. If a guy's gonna hit the ball, he's gonna hit the ball. Little bit of dirt on the ball's not going to make any difference."

"Helped tonight, didn't it?" said Frank.

"Joe Page helped tonight. That was the story."

The Mississippi Mud controversy was drawing a crowd.

"I'm not taking anything away from our relief pitcher," said Frank, "but the hitters can't see the dark balls. Look, I've seen plenty of times where the games were won or lost based on how well our guys could see the ball in the late innings."

"Get outta here. I don't believe it," said Jim.

The opinion among the crowd was split, but the tilt was definitely toward Jim Turner's "Don't make no difference" point of view.

"Don't make no difference!" said Frank in disbelief. "One of these days, I'm gonna show you guys."

Frank Crosetti was a true believer in the dark ball/light ball theory of Mississippi Mud. But like the first person who argued that the earth is round, Frank was probably just a little ahead of his time. It's hard to know when some far out baseball theory becomes a truth accepted by most ballplayers, but when I first arrived at Yankee Stadium, I ran into a number of unusual beliefs and practices. Some were strictly personal; others had gained more general acceptance.

When I started as the visiting batboy in 1949, Pete Sheehy told me "Never say no. Always try and do whatever is asked of you." So when Hank Bauer, the right fielder, asked me to nail carpet tacks into the head of his bat, I didn't think twice about it. I simply got a hammer and nails from Sheehy and went to work. A short time later, Pete introduced me to a large oven near the trainer's room.

"This is where you bake the bats." My expression said, "huh," but the words that came out of my mouth were "sure, okay." Thereafter, whenever a player wanted his bat baked, I at least knew where to do it, although, at first, I didn't know why.

Eddie Lopat, the pitching ace, had another unusual request.

"Joe, here's a chocolate covered cherry," he said one day, handing me a square box that I recognized from my neighborhood candy store.

"Thanks, Eddie, but I never eat them."

"It's not for you" he said, a rising note of surprise in his voice.

"I might be the relief pitcher today. When I come from the bullpen, you run out, I'll hand you my jacket, and you slip me the chocolate covered cherry."

"Uh...sure. Okay. Whatever you say, Eddie."

Eddie Lopat, on the down side of thirty, felt the chocolate covered cherry gave him the burst of energy he needed to get the last outs of the game. Other pitchers liked oranges, so I frequently ran to the local grocery story before the game to buy them. Between innings, Joe Page or Vic Raschi would suck the juice to the rind and get the power surge they needed. On any given day, I'd be running to a local soda shop or deli to fill special orders. Phil Rizzuto's magic elixir was a double malted milk with two scoops of ice cream and a raw egg.

Because baseball's a game of inches, every player was looking for an edge – some extra something that would help him beat the throw to first, overpower a hitter, or knock the ball into the bleachers.

Rizzuto may have hit two doubles or made a sensational double play the first time he drank his double malted. The fact that he might have been hitless in his next game, even though he used the same formula, didn't matter. Once the idea had taken hold, a player would never let go of it.

The tricks of the trade that had been accepted by most ballplayers were probably more reliable – simply because they were put to the test before they were adopted by a majority of the players.

Hank Bauer's nails, he swore, powered the ball and kept his

bat from splintering. This practice developed quite a following among other players, who found Hank's theory tried and true.

A player positively hated to lose his game bat. Early in the season, representatives of the Louisville Slugger Corporation arrived at the Stadium to take measurements for new bats. Based on such things as height, style of swing, and physical strength, a player would have about six bats custom made for himself. Of the six, a player would settle on one as his game bat, another as his practice bat, while the others were kept in reserve. Except for the pitchers, a player's sense of self-esteem may just as well have translated into his batting average. Players would to do nearly anything to hang on to a bat that was working well for them.

According to the philosophy of bat baking, an hour of slow baking dried the wood, and made it less likely to split. Hitters also swore that when they connected with a freshly baked bat, the ball jumped off the wood like a rocket.

Another bat-preservation method was "boning." This involved, first of all, a trip to the butcher for a large steak bone, which the local merchant was more than glad to donate to the Yankee cause. Once I returned to the clubhouse from the butcher, Sheehy would hammer nails through the bone into a board underneath. I took this strange looking contraption and rubbed it over the thick end of the bat for about five minutes. Boning gave the bat a nice gloss and made it less likely to splinter.

Around 1950, a combination of rosin and olive oil was gaining popularity as an improvement on the rosin bag for sweaty hands. Players would have me work the rosin and olive oil into a rag and then rub it on the handle of the bat. This mixture kept the bat from slipping when the batter came around on a pitch.

Although ballplayers could be a skeptical group, once they noticed that Ted Williams' bat handle was darkened with the sticky stuff, that ended the debate before it ever got started. Ted's bat spoke infallibly. The down side was that it created more work for the clubhouse staff, which had to scrape the build-up off the bat handle every other week or so.

Pitchers, of course, had some of their own tricks. Some would throw balls loaded with spit. The spit created an exaggerated curve ball or slider. A greasy men's hair cream, commonly used in those days, had the same effect. Either method was illegal as well as dangerous and if a player was caught doing it, he could be suspended. I don't remember any Yankee throwing spit balls, although I do remember Jim Turner telling Eddie Lopat that no one could say anything about him wiping his brow before he threw a pitch.

Without the endorsement of a Joe DiMaggio or Ted Williams, Frank Crosetti's light ball/dark theory of Mississippi Mud would have to be put to the test. The theory had to be proved during a night game in which the umpire needed more than seventy-two baseballs.

Shortly after Frank Crosetti's argument with Jim Turner, Frank finally got a chance to prove his theory. The home plate umpire had nearly exhausted his supply of balls by the top of the ninth. The Yankees trailed by a run. I could actually feel Frank's eyes on my back. I knew what he wanted me to do.

After I took my three remaining balls and gave them to the home plate umpire, I went to the clubhouse, got a dozen new baseballs, dipped into the Mississippi Mud, and wasn't at all surprised to hear, "Nice and light, Joe."

"Sure, Frank. I know."

The first batter made the Red Sox pitcher work extra hard. He fouled off three balls before drawing a walk. DiMaggio was up next. Frank, who was finally getting his chance to show the guys, had everyone on the edge of the dugout. I saw him motion to Jim Turner, as if to say, "Don't miss this one."

I knew that the umpire had one more dark ball in his pocket. Normally, I would have run up with more balls, but I knew that Frank wanted me to make sure that Joe Di would only be swinging at light-colored balls. DiMaggio fouled the first pitch into the stands. The umpire turned in my direction, but I was already by his side, giving him six light-colored balls.

The next pitch, low inside, was fouled straight away. From my spot, I could overhear some of the players saying something like, "You know, you really can see the light ball better." The next pitch was low, on the outside corner. DiMaggio caught the ball just right and it must've traveled over 400 feet to right-center – an enormous double. The run scored.

The Yankees went on to win the game, but the happiest Yankee had to be Frank Crosetti. He was gloating. He had made twenty-five true believers. Mississippi Mud was a theory no more.

11

The missing bat

Late in the 1950 season, the Yankees were involved in a three-way pennant race with the Cleveland Indians and the Red Sox. The Indians, like the Yankees, had an awesome team with a particularly fine pitching staff – including Early Wynn, Bob Feller, and Bob Lemon.

The Indians also had a heavy slugger playing third base – Al Rosen. Al was a strong, stocky player, who often hit for extra bases or home runs. While he was having a great year, Al was having an even better year against the Yankees, and was gathering a reputation around the league as a Yankee killer.

During a summer homestand with the Indians, I stumbled into a conversation about the visiting team in the Yankee clubhouse after a particularly bad game for the Yankees and a very good one for the Indians and Al Rosen.

"That Rosen fella's got our number," someone said.

"Sure does," was a reply from another Yankee.

"Keeps hitting like that, we're gonna see a pennant flying in Cleveland Stadium next year," someone else said.

I just nodded in agreement. I wasn't really part of this conversation and I just tried to skirt this small mob and find Ralph. But, strangely, this swarm of Yankee uniforms seemed to follow me. When I moved, they moved with me. Pretty soon I was in a corner, surrounded.

"I hear he's got a Yankee-slaying bat he loves more than life itself," another player chimed in.

"Sure would help us Yankees, Joe, if someone purloined that bat."

Well, "purloin" wasn't in my everyday vocabulary – or theirs either – but I had the general idea. The very thought of it gave me the cold sweats. As batboy, I observed firsthand how attached hitters were to their favorite bats, especially if they were on a streak. Pete Sheehy, who had been around the Yankee clubhouse for years, told me that Babe Ruth slept with his bat. If some of the players had to choose between their favorite bats and their wives or girlfriends, well...I had a pretty good idea who'd win that one.

At that moment, one of the Yankee "greats" came over.

"Hey, what's the matter with you guys. You're asking a fourteen-year-old boy from St. Jerome's school to steal another player's bat."

"Whew," I breathed a sigh of relief.

"Why," he said, "that's not only unethical and unsportsmanlike, it's the ultimate in bad taste."

By this point, he had put his arm around my shoulder.

"What kind of example are you guys setting for Joe?"

The pressure on my shoulder increased.

"I mean," he said, "just because it could help us win the pennant, just because his brother works in the visitor's clubhouse and he could get in there and take Rosen's bat and no one would ever be the wiser, and just because he's a Yankee like the rest of us, well...."

I looked up at him. I was speechless.

When I arrived the next afternoon I was summoned to the visitor's clubhouse. There was a thunderous commotion inside. No sooner had I opened the door than Ralph was all over me: "Joe, do you know anything about Al Rosen's bat?"

I opened my mouth but no words found their way out.

In a matter of seconds, Al Rosen, in a fury, stormed up to me, "Someone said you knew something about my bat. Where's my game bat?"

Terrified, I meekly protested, "When I left the clubhouse last night, I'm sure your bat was in the bat bag." Al looked at me with utter contempt. Like a man possessed, he tore the clubhouse apart and soon had the entire Indians team rummaging through every nook and cranny of the visitor's clubhouse for his beloved bat. It was nowhere to be found.

Al Rosen went 0 for 4 that day. The Yankees won and, not long after, the Indians were out of the pennant race.

As soon as I walked into the Yankee clubhouse after the game, at least a half dozen players ran over to me, shaking my hand, and patting me on the back, saying, "Thataboy, Joe. We knew we could count on you. You're a Yankee now."

I said not a word.

To this day, theories abound. But as long as clubhouse walls are silent, the final resting place of Al Rosen's bat remains a mystery.

12

Joe and Billy and me

I was determined to interview Joe DiMaggio and discover his definition of greatness. Finding the right moment to speak with him was never easy though.

Early in the 1950 season, my brother Ralph said to me, "You got DiMaggio in the right frame of mind. Now's a good time to ask him some questions."

It was about six o'clock and Joe had to be feeling pretty good. The Yankees won that afternoon and he hit two home runs. Almost all the other players were gone, and only the clubhouse staff remained.

When I walked up to him, Joe was sitting on a stool, with his head resting against the side of his locker. He had a cup of coffee in one hand and a cigarette in the other. He was inhaling deeply, lost somewhere in the pleasure of the moment.

"Hi Joe. Got some balls for me to sign," he said without moving.

"No Joe. Not today. I thought I'd ask you some questions. This is for a report that I have to do at school and I'd like to interview you for it."

He smiled. "You're not going to ask me what my biggest thrill was, are you Joe?"

"No," I said, laughing a bit nervously. "It's a little deeper than that. I was wondering if you could tell me what qualities you have that make you a great ballplayer."

Joe's head straightened in surprise at the question. I knew how he protected his privacy and I was afraid I might be trespassing on terrain reserved to him alone.

"I never had a question like that asked of me all the years I played baseball. Someone is always asking me what was my biggest thrill, what was my most memorable feat, or what gave me the most satisfaction – playing in the World Series or hitting in fifty-six consecutive games."

"I'll tell you what," he continued, "this is too good a question for me to just answer off the top of my head. Right now I'm kind of tired and just want to rest for a minute or two before I shower. But I promise I will think about the question and I will give you an answer."

"Okay, Joe. Thanks."

The conversation was at an end. I retreated into the trainer's room where Ralph, Pete Sheehy, Pete Previte, and Gus Mauch, the trainer, were waiting to hear what Joe Di told me.

"From the look on your face, Joe, I don't think you got your answer," Mauch said.

"No. But Joe Di said he would think about the question and get back to me."

"If he said that, then he'll do it," Sheehy said. "You'll get your answer."

"I know you didn't ask me my opinion of what makes Joe Di great," Gus Mauch said. But, in a lot of ways, I've been closer to Joe than anyone else. The way I see it, you can sum up his greatness in one word...guts. I've seen Joe play baseball with a damaged heel that would've put another player in a wheelchair. I've seen him play when his body was aching from a sore shoulder or a leg cramp that would have put a lesser man down. DiMaggio is the ultimate gutsy player. In all the years that I have been here, I have heard all kinds of complaints from players. Never once have I heard DiMaggio complain.

"Baseball is his whole life, his religion, his opium. He's not fully alive unless he has a uniform on."

"Gus is right," said Sheehy. "I never heard him complain, even though you could see the pain etched in his face. He never asked to be taken out of a game when he knew his teammates were looking to him for leadership."

Gus, who had been the Yankee trainer for twenty-five years (and who would join the New York Mets a few years later), turned to my brother. "What do you think, Ralph?"

"I just think he was born with great natural ability. Without it neither Joe nor anyone else could become outstanding.

"I've been watching him up close since 1946. That's a lot less time than you guys. But you can tell he has terrific physical qualities. He has the typical baseball physique – tall, wiry, muscular. He has a keen sense of timing, strong wrists, good eyes, and the ability to coordinate all these physical traits into one great ballplayer."

"I agree with you," said Gus. "He does have great physical characteristics. But I have been working on Joe's body longer than anybody else. There's something more that makes him a great player, because he plays well even when his body is worn and tired."

"I didn't mean to minimize his sheer determination," said Ralph.

"I think you hit the nail on the head," Gus cut him off. "That's exactly the quality that Joe has that puts him over and above everybody else. He has great determination. I have worked on all Joe's aches and pains. So often, after rubbing him down for twenty minutes, he could barely get off the table. But when the bell rings at two o'clock, he's out there giving it one hundred percent with that sheer determination, backed up by that great awareness of what a baseball game is all about."

Previte turned to me, "You started all this. What do you think?"

"I really don't have an answer yet," I said. "I've only been here a year. But based on what I've seen, I agree with everything you guys are saying. But I really want to hear what Joe has to say in his own words."

Part of Joe's mystique was that he kept so much to himself. He didn't seem to need people the way most of us do. So there was really no one to fill in the gaps for me.

I took Joe Di at his word and resolved to wait as patiently as I could for him to get back to me. I believed he would.

A few days after my conversation with Joe Di, Billy Martin, the rookie second baseman came over to me.

"Hey Joe, I hear you're asking the players about what makes them great. I got a few things to tell you."

I was making an effort to talk to the older players first and hadn't even thought about asking this first-year man about his measure of success. But I wasn't really surprised that Billy took the initiative to talk to me. No one ever called Billy shy.

"It's my physical attributes. Yeah, I got my muscles from doing a lot of boxing. That really builds up the arms and upper parts of the body," he said as he adopted a boxer's fighting stance and flexed his muscles. You gotta be strong and you gotta make the extra effort, Joe."

Both at practice and whenever Casey put him in a game, you couldn't help but notice Billy. I had never seen another player demonstrate the same level of energy and enthusiasm. He was in constant overdrive. He ran out every ground ball, no matter if it was a sure out, and he broke up many a double play by a hard slide into second. He wasn't a power hitter, but he would bear down so as to make every at bat count.

You could also tell that he was thrilled to be a Yankee. He hung on every bit of advice that Frank Crosetti or Phil Rizzuto gave him about fielding his position and he made a point of sitting next to Casey Stengel in the dugout during the games. I often caught him looking up at the crowded stands in the Stadium when he came up to bat, savoring the recognition that came his way.

What was probably most surprising about Billy, though, was the way he tagged along with Joe DiMaggio. Billy followed the great one around like a lost puppy in search of a home, waiting for a word to drop or a hint of recognition from the Yankee Clipper.

Joe needed his privacy and kept his distance from most of the players, and even from the coaches and managers. So what was even more surprising than Billy's efforts to establish a rapport with Joe Di was that Joe Di reciprocated. I had never seen anyone before Billy get this close to DiMaggio. He listened to Billy's observations and took time to answer his questions. I often wondered what Billy's secret was. He was doing what I wanted to do...only a lot more successfully.

Getting to know Joe DiMaggio was a challenge, but I befriended Billy Martin right away. Although to me Billy was a grown-up, the kid was very much alive in him and it was easy to forget that he was almost twice my age. The first time Billy asked me, "Hey Joe, how about pitching me some extra batting practice tomorrow morning early," I was a little surprised.

"Fine with me, Billy, but I better check it out with Pete."

"Pete won't mind. Bring some of your friends to shag the fly balls. Be here at 10. That'll give us an hour before the team practice."

Sheehy was a little surprised by my request. It seemed to be a first for him. Then again, Billy had given Sheehy and everyone else more than a few surprises during the 1950 season. He said, "Why not."

The next morning, Bobby and Billy Seidel and Bobby Corbo met me in front of my tenement at 9:30. They couldn't believe the offer I made them the night before and were ecstatic about the opportunity to play inside the Stadium and to meet Billy Martin. Because this was no ordinary event, we stopped first at Charlie's Hero Shop, a few blocks from home, to ensure that we'd be amply fortified for our big day. For fifteen cents each, we got a ham, salami, provolone Italian hero, smeared with hot mustard. For another dime, we got a sixteen ounce Coke, which included the two-cent deposit. It was a good deal – a man-size lunch for a quarter of a dollar.

After our walk to the Stadium, Joe Serrano opened the door for us and said, "Hi Joe. Who are these guys?"

Feeling a great sense of importance in front of my friends, I answered, "We're here to pitch and shag for Billy Martin."

"Gotta check it out with Pete," Joe said. "You know the rules."

Pete, who knew about it already, gave the green light. He even said my friends could play on the outfield grass in their sneakers. There was a blanket rule that nothing but a cleated foot was to touch the outfield grass. Pete probably figured that he had gone this far in breaking precedent, why not a little farther.

Billy was fully dressed and drinking a cup of coffee when we arrived.

"Okay guys, let's get to work," he said.

Billy admonished the Seidel brothers and Bobby Corbo, "Don't play the infield. I don't want you guys to get hurt. Just shag what I hit to the outfield."

Since I was a starting pitcher for St. Jerome's Grammar School, I felt pretty comfortable pitching to Billy. At first, I took something off my pitches, and was pitching Billy tight. He just bunted these. As I got looser, I started to groove the ball over the plate. Billy started whacking them into deep right center field. The shots were going anywhere from 300 to 350 feet. I was surprised by Billy's power. He wasn't big or bulky, but he used his entire body, coiled like a cobra, coordinating each muscle. He had a way of springing into the ball, his sheer energy compensating for any lack of natural power.

I got so involved in throwing my fast ball over home plate that I didn't react on a line drive smacked right at me. The ball caromed off my left elbow and I hit the dirt. The pain was excruciating. Billy's face was a sickly white by the time he reached the mound.

"You okay?"

"Sure," I said.

"Why don't we go get some ice from Pete?"

"No way. I'm fine. Really."

Billy didn't put up too much of an argument. I think the last thing he wanted was to go back and tell Casey that he had put the ballboy out of commission.

I got back in my pitching groove, which seemed to take my mind off the pain. I kept pitching for another twenty minutes or so.

When we were finished, Billy took us back to the clubhouse, bought us Cokes, and gave each of us five dollars. My friends were excited beyond belief. Billy knew how to develop a following.

It was now after eleven o'clock and many of the players were drifting in. Sheehy gave the high sign that it was time for my friends to go.

Billy must've noticed because he asked the guys if they were staying for the game. "No. We don't have tickets," said Bobby Corbo.

"I'll take care of that," Billy said, motioning for them to follow him.

As my friends told me later, Billy took the boys to Charlie King, the head usher, and asked Charlie to set them up in box seats. I think from that day on my friends were among Billy's most devoted admirers.

I was beginning my chores when Billy walked back in.

"You sure you're okay, Joe?" he asked.

"Just fine. Thanks for everything. The guys were thrilled to be here. They won't ever forget you."

"Hey, they did me a favor."

Just then, Casey Stengel walked in. "How come you're all sweated up, Martin?" Casey asked. "We haven't even started practice."

"I came early. Joe and his friends were giving me a little extra batting practice."

"Is that right? I guess you're feeling pretty strong?"

"Yeah, Coach," Billy said, "I am feeling pretty strong. But I gotta keep my strength up. Did I ever tell you how I got my upper body strength from boxing? Well, let me tell you about that, coach."

I smiled broadly, but the pain in my arm pinched. A reminder. It was time to get back to work.

13

Fathers and sons

Just before the start of a night game, Casey Stengel pulled me aside as I was about to run out of the dugout to my stool along the first base line.

"Joe, what high school are you going to attend in September?"

"Cardinal Hayes," I answered.

"That so."

"Yeah. It's right on 153rd Street and the Grand Concourse. I can run through Francez Sigel Park and get to the Stadium in five minutes.

"Yes, I know you're going to Cardinal Hayes," Casey said.

If it were someone other than Casey, I might have wondered why he asked a question that he already had an answer for. But, as I had learned over the prior eighteen months, there was no point in trying to follow Casey's logic.

"I know Monsignor Waterson, the Dean at Cardinal Hayes. We were talking about you the other night. I guess you are a little concerned about whether they'll let you out of school for the afternoon games?"

"Gee, Casey, you must've been reading my mind," I said. "My principal at St. Jerome's has been great about letting me out, but I heard Monsignor Waterson is pretty strict. I haven't even figured out how I'm going to bring it up with him."

"Don't worry about that, Joe. The dean and I were sitting on the dais together at a testimonial dinner at the Grand Concourse Hotel. He knows you're coming to Cardinal Hayes and I told him 'watch out for Joe. He is a Yankee. Take good care of him.' The monsignor told me there was going to be no problem. He will make sure that you will be let go from your classes to get to the afternoon games."

"I don't how to thank you, Casey."

"Joe, I consider the Yankees my family, and you are part of that family. As long as I'm here, you'll be here."

I was amazed. I hadn't even asked Casey for his help, but the manager of the World Champion Yankees made it his business to ease me past the one obstacle that could have short-circuited my career with the team.

Casey Stengel's tortured diction (which reminded me of Mugsy on the Dead End Kids) and wandering discourses, made great copy for the sportswriters, who delighted New York's baseball fans with stories of the Ol' Perfesser. But there was another Casey – the paterfamilias, the one who loved his children, guided them through troubled waters, and tried to protect them from every harm. If you were part of his family, whether you were the batboy, the clubhouse man, or the newest player on the team, he'd adopt you and look out for your best interests.

When I first met him, Casey was sixtyish, short and bulky, with a pointed nose, thick curly white hair, a ready smile, a quick wit, and a good word for all the new guys. He could've been your dad or your favorite uncle. And with so many young players on the team, many in their early twenties, he was the father figure who would ease their transition to the major leagues or maybe even to stardom.

During the 1950 season, I often observed young players go into Casey's office after a game. Sometimes he'd holler, "Hey Martin, come in here." On other occasions, some young player with the world on his shoulders would tap lightly on the door to his office and ask, "Casey, have you got a few minutes?" The answer was always the same. "Of course. Come on in."

Inevitably, after a twenty or thirty minute chat with "Dad," the rookie left his anxiety inside with Casey and returned to the world with a smile on his face. As these players related their conversations, no matter what the problem, whether it was a shortage of money, the rookie jitters, or a painful divorce, Casey was there to help. If there was a death in the family, Casey would comfort the player, telling him, "We'll miss you for the next few days, but your place is with your family. Go with a clear mind. Don't worry about baseball. You'll be missed, but when you come back, we'll be here with open arms."

As much as Casey was fond of the younger players, he seemed to keep his distance from the veterans. I often overheard Casey commenting to his coaches about the next generation of Yankees. His eyes were focused on the future. If he was beholden to the veterans for winning the 1949 World Series, he didn't show it.

In 1950, Phil Rizzuto was at the height of his career. He hit .324, his defensive play was nearly perfect, and his team spirit was a decisive factor in helping the Yankees capture their second straight pennant. Phil finally got the recognition he so richly deserved, being named the American League's Most Valuable Player. But even Phil was not beyond Casey's reproach. Once, Phil failed to execute a play according to Casey's directions and I thought Casey was going to bite his head off. Phil just sucked it in and never said a word in the dugout. Back inside the clubhouse though, he said to me, "Did you hear how he talked to me?"

"Oh, he didn't mean it, Phil," I responded, trying to cheer up my friend.

"He *did* mean it," Phil fired back.

I backed off quickly. I had never seen the ever-friendly Rizzuto snap like that, although I knew that he often felt unappreciated by the Yankee manager.

The distance between Joe Di and Casey was even more pronounced. I picked up right away that these two never spoke more than a word or two to each other. Casey never seemed awed by DiMaggio as did nearly everyone else. Neither did he express any criticism. It was as if these two big, important people in my life existed at opposite poles of an unbridgeable gulf.

I liked Casey and worshiped DiMaggio. Fortunately, I was never put in a position where I had to choose between the two of them. That would've been hard, if not impossible, for me to resolve. But maybe Casey realized that to force anyone to take sides on a team would have been divisive. It was his job to keep his family together, and he seemed to have developed his own methods of doing that.

In contrast to the funny man who told jokes, played the clown, and spoke Stengelese for the sportswriters, Casey was brilliant as a manager. If Casey didn't invent the two-platoon system, he brought it to a point of perfection that was the envy of every team in the league. If the opposing team was going with a right-handed pitcher, he would put in a left-handed first baseman like Joe Collins or Johnny Mize. If the opposing pitcher was left-handed, it might be Johnny Hopp. He used the same strategy in the outfield, platooning Hank Bauer with Gene Woodling. Snuffy Stirnweiss and Jerry Coleman took turns playing second base. The two-platoon system was a sore point for the veterans, who undoubtedly wanted to play every day, but it provided a great opportunity for the up-and-coming players like Billy Martin.

Casey had taken a strong liking to Billy, in no small part because Billy worshiped him like a father. They became so close that a clubhouse joke was, "Where's Billy's father?" meaning of course, "Where's Casey Stengel?"

Shortly after I met him, Billy told me he had come from a broken home. His mother divorced when he was young and he was raised, more or less, by his grandmother.

"What I know, I learned in the streets," Billy once told me. "Everything I have I had to fight for. Nothing was given to me. I got into enough fights so that I know how to take care of myself."

Tough as he was, though, Billy looked to Casey as the father he never had for guidance and encouragement. Casey took him under his wing. On the bench, Billy would sit right next to Casey and, like a sponge, absorb everything the old man had to say. Billy would ask questions, he would listen, he would observe, and he always showed Casey the utmost respect.

"The players can't believe that Casey and I have so much in common that we talk constantly," Billy said.

"What they don't realize is that the only real difference between Casey and me is that Casey is sixty and I'm twenty-two. Otherwise, we're a lot alike. I'm brash and talkative. So is he. I take chances and I feel nothing succeeds like success. I'll do anything to win. You can say the same about Casey. I feel that the sky's the limit. There are no barriers we can't overcome. So does Casey. And you know what Joe…someday, just like Casey, I'm going to be the manager of the New York Yankees."

Billy's bravado caused me to think of my own father. He was the quiet man…so unlike either Casey or Billy. When you have a good father, it's easy to take him for granted. I don't think I ever realized what I had until, at age fourteen, I met someone like Billy Martin who told me what it was like to grow up on your own. Although I always appreciated Casey's kindnesses, I would never need him the way Billy did.

When my father wasn't working at the U.S. Army Base in Brooklyn, he was with his family. He frequently sat with me on the stoop of our apartment building as I did my homework…sometimes for hours at a stretch. He didn't say much, except to tell me not to work so hard and go have some fun. If he never said a word though, I always felt his presence and support.

Although he was not an athlete and never played baseball, I first played the game with my dad. Often on summer weekends my mom packed a picnic lunch and the family took the Jerome Avenue train to Woodlawn Park in the Bronx. We'd find an open field where Ralph would pitch, I would hit, and my dad played the outfield. We played until we were ready to drop and then relaxed in the shade, drinking Mom's cool lemonade and enjoying her baked lasagna and fried chicken. Although he wasn't a baseball fan, my dad grew to love the Yankees when Ralph became the ballboy. He made sure that our family was one of the first in the neighborhood to buy a television so that we could all see Ralph perform his duties at Yankee Stadium.

My father spoke volumes in a matter of words – words that

seemed to stay with you. When I started with the Yankees, he said to me, "A lot of people are putting their trust in you. Don't let us down. When you are with the Yankees, you are with famous and powerful people. I would advise that you let it all happen gradually. Don't be aggressive. Be a good listener and don't talk too much. But always remember, stand up for what you believe in. When you are right, don't back down. No matter what happens, your mother and father will always believe in you."

My father was born in Cosenza, Amendolda, Calabria, Italy. He explained that Cosenza is the village, Amendolda the town, and Calabria the province. He was only fourteen – about the same age as me when I started at Yankee Stadium – when he came to America to live with his father. My grandfather had come ahead of his family to start a new life here. My father liked to tell a story that as a young man working at a construction site with his father he slipped into an excavation and was buried under six feet of sand and gravel. While someone ran to tell my grandfather, who was working close by, the other laborers tried frantically to unearth my father. In no time at all my grandfather arrived, shoved everyone out of his way, and with an extraordinary effort, he unearthed my father and saved his life.

I always knew my father would have done the same for me. What more could a son ask for?

14

A dream come true

I once told Brother Colombo that my goal in life was to become the Yankee batboy. When he asked why, I told him that it was a really important job. You are the keeper of a player's most important tool. You get to know the players as individuals because you have to talk to them about what bat they'll use at practice, what bat they'll use in the game, how they like their bat dressed for a better grip – whether in pine tar or rosin.

During my first year with the Yankees when I was the batboy for the visiting teams, Ted Williams broke his bat during a game. He left it up to me to run back to the dugout and pick another one out of the rack for him. When I brought it out in front of a big crowd at the ballpark, he looked it up and down, and then nodded his head. That's recognition. If I could do that for Ted Williams of the Boston Red Sox, I knew I could do it for Joe DiMaggio of the New York Yankees.

I also told Brother Colombo about the perquisites of the batboy position. Although the pay wasn't any better (pay for both batboy and ballboy positions was a dollar a game), batboy was a high status job that provided a better opportunity to get to know the players well. The batboy also traveled with the team on a lengthy road trip every summer. As a kid who had hardly ever been out of the Bronx, I couldn't wait to travel with the World Champion Yankees and to be greeted by cheering fans in places like Boston, Washington, Cleveland, and Detroit.

Becoming the Yankee batboy would also provide my last, best chance to get to know Joe Di. Like a page to a medieval knight, I was at his beck and call. Since I had to hand a player his bat three or four times a game, I had the kind of access that would allow me finally to complete my quest. I wanted to befriend DiMaggio or at least to get to know him as best I could before he retired. I wanted him to answer my question about the secret of his success – to tell me in his own words what made him great.

When the 1950 season ended, I still had one more rung to climb before I reached the top of the clubhouse ladder. It didn't seem that I would climb that rung anytime soon though. The batboy, Bert Padell, had been with the Yankees only a year. Usually, the Yankee batboy stayed in that position for at least three or four seasons. By the time Bert left, DiMaggio would probably be gone as well.

I wouldn't let discouragement creep in though. I knew what my goal was so I made a sincere effort to do it right as the ballboy – with just a few slips – in the hope that a good performance as ballboy would help me graduate to the next level.

The biggest part of the ballboy's job was to run down foul balls as quickly as possible so that they didn't interrupt the flow of the game. Because I was fast, I did a good job chasing balls down the first and third base lines, or catching them off the screen behind home plate. There was a tradition of sorts that any ballboy worth his pinstripes would never let a ball roll off the screen and hit the dirt.

I never had a problem keeping this venerable tradition alive.

Early in the season, though, at the urging of a fun-loving kid named Phil Rizzuto, I hesitated before I ran to catch a Johnny Mize foul ball off the screen. At the last second, I dashed from my stool outside the Yankee dugout and made a shoestring catch. The fans behind home plate were delighted. They gave me a big cheer and I took a bow. I trotted back to the dugout to the applause of Rizzuto, Tommy Henrich, Doc Brown and several others. I even caught Casey Stengel with the glimmer of a smile on his face. Frank Crosetti's angry stare could've cut me in half though. To Frank, the baseball purist, I was hotdogging it, providing an annoying distraction to the game. I got the message. It was a good performance, but one I rarely, if ever, repeated.

1950 was a great year for the Yankees. Although they finished only three games ahead of the Detroit Tigers, the pennant race was never really in doubt. The Yankees received stellar performances from Vic Raschi, Phil Rizzuto, Yogi Berra, Eddie Lopat, Joe DiMaggio, and Johnny "Big Cat" Mize.

The Big Cat, at the end of a great career, had a comeback season, hitting 25 home runs. Joe Di hit .301, and although not the Joe of old, his statistics were enviable. He batted in 122 runs, and hit 32 homers. Eddie Lopat, the "junk man," whose off-speed pitches drove batters crazy, won 18 games, lost only 8, and finished 15. Yogi Berra hit .322, becoming the Yankees' steady catcher and earning the respect of every player in the league as a great, natural hitter. Phil Rizzuto, the Yankees' heart, hit .324 and was named the American League's Most Valuable Player. Vic Raschi, a venerable professor of pitching science, won 21 games and lost only 8.

Other Yankee standouts included Hank Bauer, who batted

.320, and Jerry Coleman who wrested the steady second baseman slot from George "Snuffy" Stirnweiss. Jerry hit .287 for the year, not bad for a second baseman, and made famous his patented choke grip, exposing the bottom four inches of the bat handle.

The Yankees took the World Series in four straight games over a tough Philadelphia squad. Although three of the four victories were by only one run, because of the Yankee pitching the games never seemed quite as close as the final tallies indicated.

In Game One in Philadelphia, Vic Raschi needed only one run, as he shut out the Phillies. Jim Konstanty – their starter – had been a relief pitcher all season. He surprised everyone by pitching a great game. The Yankees were just a little bit better. In Game Two, Allie Reynolds pitched a complete game, giving up only one run in ten innings. The game's great moment was a tenth inning home run by the Yankee Clipper that provided the margin of victory as the Yankees took it 2 to 1. My only disappointment was that I wasn't in Philadelphia to share in Joe Di's great moment.

The teams returned to New York for Game Three. This time, Eddie Lopat gave up only two runs on seven hits as New York won 3 to 2.

In the fourth and final game of the Series on October 7th, a rookie named Whitey Ford won his first of eight career World Series victories. Whitey – a local boy from Queens, New York – came up in the middle of the 1950 season and dazzled the baseball world with nine consecutive victories. Not bad for a rookie. In his first World Series start, Whitey held the Phillies scoreless until the 9th inning when Gene Woodling dropped a fly ball with two out, allowing two unearned runs. Taking no chances,

Casey Stengel called in his ace – Allie Reynolds – who struck out the last batter to end the game.

The 1950 Series showed that the Yankees were building a dynasty on the strength of their pitching. Jim Turner, the pitching coach, not only had great hurlers, his conditioning techniques, which involved a great deal of running, developed pitchers with great endurance. Aside from the relief appearance by Reynolds in Game Four of the Series, the only other reliever to make an appearance was Tom Ferrick. He pitched one inning of relief in Game Three. Only the inhabitants of the Yankee bullpen were disappointed by this show of pitching brilliance.

After every World Series victory during this era, the Yankees had a lavish party. In 1950, it was held at the Hotel Edison in Manhattan. The clubhouse staff, from Pete Sheehy to the visiting batboy, was invited to join the team and the Yankee management. Ralph, Bert Padell – the Yankee batboy, and I attended, but Pete Sheehy never showed up. This had happened the year before, so no one was surprised by Pete's absence. He had told me more than once that he didn't like to socialize with the players.

Pete's view of the world was circumscribed by the four walls of the clubhouse. It wasn't often that I saw him out in the open, in the light of day. He did come into the dugout, but never past the top step. I don't ever remember him taking the field.

He ruled the clubhouse though. Although he was there for the players' benefit, he was in charge and his presence and authority were felt in every corner of the place. Pete had a keen sense of where he fit in the scheme of things. He knew his place and expected other people to know theirs, whether a baseball player or a ballboy. Although the batboys and ballboy reported to Pete, they spent a good portion of their time away from him on the field with the World Champion Yankees. Because we were in the limelight, it was easy to forget that picking up dirty laundry, shining shoes, and running to the local deli were, in Pete's view, equally important parts of the job. Some of them did forget. I never did.

Attitude counted for a lot with Pete. One of the first times I met him, he said, "Do whatever is asked of you. If you can't do it, at least try, and someone will appreciate that you made the effort." That was his creed and he had little tolerance for people who didn't share the same belief.

Pete thought highly of my brother Ralph. From my first day at Yankee Stadium, he let me know that Ralph had begun a Carrieri tradition that I was expected to live up to. I knew that Pete's respect for Ralph was based not so much on Ralph's abilities, which were considerable, but on his attitude.

In my quest to define greatness, George Stirnweiss, who finished his Yankee career in 1950, told me that attitude was the key ingredient to a successful life.

George said, "To be a success in any field, Joe, you have to have the proper attitude. You have to learn how to get along with people. The people on top aren't necessarily the brightest or hardest working, but they know how to get along with other people."

Pete's tenure as clubhouse man spanned half a century, from Babe Ruth to Reggie Jackson. And the key to his longevity was attitude. You could observe it in the way Pete related to baseball's greatest players. As close as he was to them, he kept a respectful distance so that the players never took him or his position within the Yankee organization for granted.

Shortly after the 1950 World Series, I returned to the clubhouse to help Pete pack up for the winter. Much to my surprise, Pete told me that Bert Padell was leaving.

"He's going to a an out-of-town college," said Pete.

"You're kidding!"

"Don't get your hopes up," said Pete, who knew what I was thinking.

"A Congressman called the front office. He wants to line up the job for his friend's son. There's a lot of pressure on me to take this kid. It's even coming from George Weiss himself."

George Weiss, the General Manager, ran the Yankee organization like a supreme potentate. Ultimately, he was in charge of hiring and firing, from Joe DiMaggio to the Yankee batboy.

"If I don't become the batboy, Pete, I understand," I said, trying to take some of the pressure off him.

"Well, I don't understand. It's just not going to happen," he shouted. I had rarely seen Pete get angry, but his anger wasn't directed toward me.

He dropped what he was doing, picked up the phone and called Red Patterson, the publicity chief who was handling the matter for Mr. Weiss. Pete was shouting into the phone. He slammed down the receiver and returned to his work with a sullen vengeance. In a matter of minutes Patterson appeared. He was surprised that I was in the clubhouse. He whispered something to Pete so that I wouldn't hear him, but Pete said sternly, "No, we're going to talk now, and we're going to talk in front of Joe."

"Pete, this is a direct order from George Weiss. He said the batboy position goes to the Congressman's friend."

"Look," answered Pete, "this has been tried before and it didn't work. The batboy has to be trained and he has to work his way into the position. He's got to get to know his way around the players. He's got to learn what they do and don't like, how to fit it, how not to interfere with the game. Some new kid is not going to know all that and if he didn't earn the position, he's not going to want to learn it."

"Pete, this is politics. This Congressman can make it tough for the Yankees. You don't have to think about these things, but George Weiss does and so do I."

"Joe should be the new batboy," Pete said. He's earned it and he knows the job."

I could hardly believe what I was hearing.

Patterson was irresistible force; Pete immovable object. It was then that Pete resorted to the big bomb.

"Look Red, if you want this kid so bad, then find yourself a new man. Because I'll quit, so help me God."

Well that did it. Patterson was stunned.

"Why don't we go tell that to George Weiss?"

"Fine with me," said Pete.

They were gone for the longest half-hour of my life. As I sat and waited, it seemed that everything I had hoped for or dreamed about since I started with the Yankees hung in the balance. I tried to rationalize what I was feeling, telling myself that if I didn't become the batboy another opportunity would come along. But I had a lot riding on this. It was what I wanted more than anything and there was no way that I could turn off the feelings. If I didn't get the job, I was going to be terribly disappointed.

When, finally, Pete returned, he wore an angry scowl as he walked right past me without saying a word. My heart sank.

In a moment, he was back with a Ballantine in one hand

Age 16, Yankee batboy showing off baseball's most powerful arsenal at Yankee Stadium in 1952.

With Casey Stengel during a game.

Ralph Carrieri in 1948, age 17

Ralph Carrieri, in the windbreaker, with the victorious 1949 World Champions.

Ralph Carrieri, Yankee batboy, and Joe Carrieri on his first day as visiting batboy, 1949.

Joe Carrieri, Yankee batboy, in 1951.

Joe Carrieri, Yankee batboy, congratulating Yogi Berra after he hits a home run. Irv Noren, number 25, is in the foreground.

Joe Carrieri behind his desk at Carrieri & Carrieri.

Joe Carrieri, at an adoption in 1994 at the Surrogate's Court, Nassau County. Judge Raymond C. Radigan is seated at left. Clerk Sandy Schwartz is also present.

National Baseball Library, Cooperstown, New York

Ralph Carrieri, front left with the 1947 World Champions

National Baseball Library, Cooperstown, New York

Ralph Carrieri, Yankee batboy, front right with the 1949 World Champions

Joe Carrieri in his first year as Yankee ballboy, front right with the 1950 World Champions

National Baseball Library, Cooperstown, New York

Joe Carrieri in his first year as Yankee batboy, with the 1951 World Champions

Back row: Allie Reynolds, Johnny Mize, Gil McDougald, Ernie Nevel, Bob Kuzava, Frank Shea, Johnny Sain, Tom Morgan, Clint Courtney, Ralph Houk, Joe DiMaggio, Frank Overmire.

Second row: Gus Mauch (trainer), Jim Brideweser, Archie Wilson, Jerry Coleman, Bobby Brown, Johnny Hopp, Hank Bauer, Mickey Mantle, Jackie Jensen, Joe Ostrowski, Joe Collins, Vic Raschi.

Front row: Larry Berra, Phil Rizzuto, Billy Martin, Ed Lopat, Tom Henrich, Jim Turner (coach), Casey Stengel (manager), Frank Crosetti (coach), Bill Dickey (coach), Bob Hogue (coach), Art Schallock, Gene Woodling, Charles Silvera.

Batboys: Joe Carrieri, Joe Call.

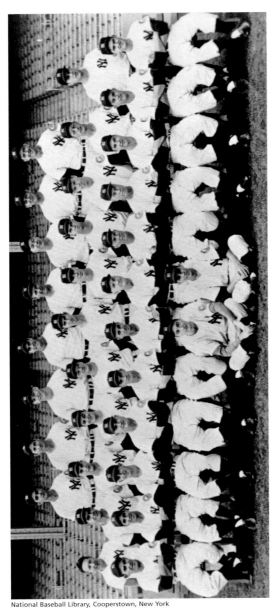

National Baseball Library, Cooperstown, New York

Joe Carrieri in his second year as Yankee batboy, with the 1952 Yankees in their fourth straight year as World Champions

Back row: Loren Rabe, Rae Scarborough, Mickey Mantle, Hank Bauer, Ralph Houk, Ed Lopat, Allie Reynolds, Joe Collins.

Second row: Gus Mauch (trainer), Charlie Keller, Jim Brideweser, Bill Miller, Tom Gorman, Ewell Blackwell, Bob Kuzava, Johnny Sain, Gil McDougald, Joe Ostrowski, Vic Raschi.

Front row: Larry Berra, Phil Rizzuto, Billy Martin, Johnny Mize, Irv Noren, Frank Crosetti (coach), Casey Stengel (manager), Bill Dickey (coach), Jim Turner (coach), Bob Hogue (coach), Jim McDonald, Gene Woodling, Charlie Silvera.

Batboys: Joe Carrieri, Iggy Manzidelis.

National Baseball Library, Cooperstown, New York

1953 World Champions

Back row: Johnny Mize, Ed Lopat, Andy Carey, Mickey Mantle, Hank Bauer, Ralph Houk, Johnny Sain, Don Bollweg, Allie Reynolds, Joe Collins.

Second row: Gus Mauch (trainer), Jim McDonald, Willie Miranda, Jerry Coleman, Bob Kuzava, Bill Miller, Tom Gorman, Bill Renna, Gus Triandos, Vic Raschi.

Front row: Art Schallock, Whitey Ford, Billy Martin, Phil Rizzuto, Larry Berra, Steve Kraly, Frank Crosetti (coach), Casey Stengel (manager), Bill Dickey (coach), Jim Turner (coach), Bob Hogue (coach), Gil McDougald, Irv Noren, Gene Woodling, Charlie Silvera.

Bat Boys: Joe Carrieri, Iggy Manzidelis.

The Carrieri family in 1994

Left to right: Donald McIntosh, son-in-law; Marilyn McIntosh, daughter; Chris Carrieri, son; Michael Carrieri, son; Jessica Carrieri, daughter; Joe Carrieri; Marilyn Carrieri, wife; Steve Carrieri, son; Joe Carrieri, Jr., son.

and a Coke in the other. He slammed the soda bottle on the table in front of me and said, "Welcome aboard, Yankee batboy."

My mouth dropped. I couldn't believe my ears.

"Joe, you earned it."

After his toast, Pete said, "Come here. I want to show you something special."

He took me into a room in a remote corner of the clubhouse. I had seen the door but I had never been through it. It was always locked and Pete had the only key.

Pete unlocked the door and turned on the light, illuminating a huge room about 20 x 40 feet. The room was filled with big trunks, stacked one on top of another. It was dank and dusty and had the look and feel of an antique shop.

"What's in here, Pete?"

"This, Joe, is our safe room. Since fans will try and steal just about anything belonging to a famous ballplayer, I need a spot to leave things where no one can get to them. It's my secret – my hideaway. The guys are always giving me something. 'Take care of this Pete. I don't want to lose it.' So I just put whatever it is in here so as not to have to worry about it. Now that you're the batboy, I'll be sending you here for things. So, make yourself familiar with this place."

"What's in the trunks?"

"Just about anything you can imagine. Bats, balls, uniforms, spikes, socks. We got some great souvenirs in here as well… autographed bats that belonged to Babe Ruth, Lou Gehrig, Tony Lazerri; old gloves belonging to Dizzy Dean and Bill Dickey; baseballs autographed by Ty Cobb. We have bats for every player on the roster in case a player loses his game bat or practice bat. Nobody goes in this room without my say so."

"Well," said Pete, "you deserve a gift for your promotion. Treat yourself."

"Anything I want?"

"Go ahead."

"Where do you keep the old bats?"

Pete took me right to a particular trunk. "Help me lift it down," he said.

We got on either end of the trunk and lowered it to the floor. I threw open the latches and opened up the treasure chest. There were more bats than I had ever seen. I rummaged through, reading name after name until my search ended with the magic words.

"Here's the one I was looking for." I held it up to the light to be sure that it was, in fact, a DiMaggio signature.

"Think he'll ever use it? I asked."

"It's yours."

"You're sure," I said.

"Absolutely. This is your day. Go find one for your brother as well."

So I dug a little further until I came upon a Phil Rizzuto signature.

"Ralph will like this. Has he ever been in here?" I asked.

Ralph was never the batboy.

"Maybe I won't tell him where I got it. But he's going to like it no matter what."

I closed up the trunk and Pete and I returned it to its resting place. I closed the light and Pete locked the door behind him.

When I was finally ready to leave, two bats over my shoulder, I thanked Pete one more time.

"You didn't have to out on a limb for me, Pete."

"Sure I did. It'll make my life a whole lot easier."

"I'll see you come spring."

"I hope you stop by before then," Pete answered.

"You know I will. I always do. This is my second home."

Pete smiled. He knew that feeling all too well.

I left him and walked home, trophies in hand...a wealthy, proud young man...living proof that dreams really do come true.

15

Natural talent

Brother Colombo often said that we're all naturally good at something. When I was thirteen or fourteen, I thought I knew what that "something" was. I was a baseball player and I planned to ply my trade with the New York Yankees – someday. Whenever I wasn't working at the Yankee clubhouse, if the weather was right I was outside playing baseball. It wasn't unusual for my friends and me to play for eight hours at a stretch on Randall's Island in New York's East River or Harvey's Hill Park in my South Bronx neighborhood. After school and on the weekends, I was the starting pitcher for my grammar school. When I got to Cardinal Hayes High, I switched to the outfield, in no small part because I could hit and I wanted to play every game. I wasn't a superstar, but I knew I had talent.

I also had a distinct advantage. I was working with the greatest baseball players of a generation and I had been commissioned by Brother Colombo to define the secrets of their success. This was no longer an academic exercise but an obsession that I used to help me achieve my long sought after goal.

I once asked Phil Rizzuto the secret to his success. Never at a loss for words or a few moments to spare, Phil said, "Joe, that's easy. When you're my height, you just have to try harder. In order to keep up with these 6'2" strong guys with the big muscles, I had to compensate and be better in other areas. I knew I'd never be a slugger, but I practiced bunting and worked on my fielding until I felt I couldn't get much better at it."

Phil did a lot of small things extraordinarily well. His patented bunt was one of them. Phil didn't square off to bunt like most hitters, but remained in a hitter's stance to the last split second before his bat hit the ball. In one fluid motion, he'd drop the bat to his side and lay down a bunt along the first or third base line, catching the infielders off balance. Inevitably, the bunt to third found the third baseman too far back and the bunt to first pulled the first baseman off the bag. Before an infielder could fire the ball or the pitcher could cover the bag, Phil was standing on first with a single.

The diminutive Rizzuto, only 5'6", was the smallest player on the Yankees and probably the smallest man in all of baseball. But was he fast. The Scooter – his legs spinning, his head always up. He not only darted around the bases, he was one of the game's all-time great defensive players. He executed the double play with amazing grace and was famous for going into the hole between short and third, making a back-handed stab, jumping high in the air and throwing the runner out at first base by half a foot.

"If you want to play baseball, Joe, you'll have to specialize and become the best there is in a particular area. How old are you?"

"Fifteen."

"Well, if I was your age and I thought that I'd like to be a major league ballplayer, I'd try to develop myself as a catcher. A catcher is not expected to hit .300, but if he is smart and works at this craft, he will become valuable simply because a smart catcher who can handle pitchers is hard to find. But kids don't want to wear a mask, chest protector, and shin guards. They would rather play the outfield and catch all the balls and all the glory. But outfielders are a dime a dozen and you better hit .320 to make the grade."

Phil was always a positive, a plus, a person with an optimistic point of view. DiMaggio won games with his bat, with his fielding, and even with his running. Rizzuto won games not by sheer power, but by contributing an intangible psychological and emotional presence that drew the best out in his teammates.

In the early 1950s, with many of the older players like DiMaggio and Henrich close to retirement and players like Mantle, Martin, and Berra beginning their careers, Phil bridged the gap between the generations. He revered the Yankee tradition of excellence, which the older players represented, and he encouraged the younger players to keep it going. Ever the diplomat, on-field and off, he once broke up a heated argument between Billy and Yogi. Phil came over, put his arm around Billy, and said, "Come on Billy. You have to respect your elders," he said jokingly, since Yogi was only a couple of years older than Billy. "Let's shake hands and make up." He walked Billy over, got him to shake Yogi's hand, and the argument was at an end. For the Yankees, little things like that made all the difference.

When I told Phil I was going to Cardinal Hayes High, he said "Great! It's got a excellent reputation. You're a smart kid. Get a good education and you can become a doctor or lawyer."

I'd rather play for the Yankees," I said.

"You can do that too," he offered with a smile. "But get an

education first. In the long run, it'll pay off."

"You sound like my mom," I said.

"That's okay. Your mother is a very intelligent woman."

Hardly a day went by that Phil and I didn't exchange at least a few words. He loved to give advice and we often talked about what I was learning from the baseball players I observed and spoke to. Toward the end of the 1950 season, he told me to make sure I spoke to Tommy Henrich and Joe Page before the end of the year. Phil sensed as did most of the veterans that Casey had plans to ease out his older players in favor of the next generation of Yankees. Casey's system of platooning, which forced the aging team members to share playing time with his rising stars, foreshadowed the changes to come. It didn't happen all at once, but each year the stars of the 1940s were traded or called it quits. For players like Charlie Keller, George Stirnweiss, Joe Page, and Tommy Henrich, the October ending to their careers was bittersweet. Although these men of autumn finished their playing days on a World Series team, they saw the sun setting on their careers as it rose on those of Billy Martin, Mickey Mantle, Whitey Ford, and Jerry Coleman. Phil knew that neither Page nor Henrich had much time left with the team and he wanted me to speak to them while I had the opportunity.

Joe Page, the Yankees' star reliever in the late 1940s, was always friendly and approachable, so I didn't hesitate to ask him about the secret of his success. Joe remained upbeat even though his stats had rapidly deteriorated. In 1949, he won thirteen games and saved twenty-seven. In 1950, he won three, lost seven, and saved only thirteen games.

"Joe," he said, "there's a bunch of reasons I think I succeeded.

125

I love the game of baseball. I love to play it, and I relish the excitement of coming in at crucial moments and 'putting out the fire.'"

"Well," I asked, "if you had to explain your success in a syllable or two, what word would you use?"

"Concentration."

"Why's that?"

"When you're in the bullpen waiting to be called to relieve a pitcher who may be tiring or in trouble, your entire focus is on the next batter you have to face. I try and empty my mind of every distraction to such a point that even if there's 60,000 noisy fans, I don't hear a sound. I give my full attention to the task at hand, which is to get the next batter out. As far as I'm concerned, there's only three people in Yankee Stadium – the batter, the catcher, and me. I concentrate on Yogi's signals. If I don't like what I see, I shake him off. Once Yogi and I agree on the pitch, I focus my full attention on the batter, his stance, how far the from the plate he plants his feet, the position of his arms, his shoulders, the bat. Then, by some mental process, I determine how fast, how wide, or how low I'll place the pitch."

"I agree with Joe Page up to a point," said Frank Shea, a younger starting pitcher who still had some years left with the Yankees. Frank had been listening in and, as often happened with the players, he eased his way into the middle of the conversation.

"You have to focus and concentrate on the task at hand, whether it's striking out the batter or making him hit into a double play. But I don't think Page's response really answers your question.

"I think a successful ballplayer must have other qualities

first, before you consider whether or not he has the ability to concentrate. He must have the right motivation and persistence or he'll never get past his first year in the minor leagues. To become a major league baseball player is not an easy road. There's hardly a man in this clubhouse who didn't ride hundreds of miles on a bus, traveling from city to city to play the next three-game series, living in the cheapest motels along the way.

"If a ballplayer doesn't have motivation, the first time he hits an obstacle, he'll quit. I don't know how often I wanted to hang up my glove. But always my motivation was to be a Yankee and I wasn't going to stop, and I wasn't going to quit no matter how hard it was, until I became a Yankee."

Another day, I sought out Tommy Henrich – "Old Reliable." Tommy was famous for his clutch hitting and for picking up the slack when one of his teammates was injured or in a slump. In 1949, his timely hits and great catches helped sustain the Yankee drive to the American League pennant and World Series when the Yankees played without a healthy Joe DiMaggio for a good part of the season.

Tommy was thirty-seven years old in 1950 and in one short year his playing time had been cut substantially by Casey. He played in 115 games in 1949 but only 73 in 1950. In 1949, he hit 24 home runs and batted in 85 runs. The following year he hit just 6 homers and batted in only 34 runs.

"I am going to tell you what I consider a secret," Tommy said. "Many people say 'practice, practice, practice' and 'practice makes perfect.' That's only half right. If you are not doing it right to begin with, practice will only compound the error.

"In order to be a success at hitting, you have to determine what's the best way to hit a fast ball, the curve, a knuckle ball or slider. When you know how to react to each pitch, practice what you have learned.

"Learn how to do it right initially, then practice until it becomes perfection."

Both Joe Page and Charlie Henrich finished their Yankee careers in 1950 as did George Stirnweiss, who had been a good friend to my brother Ralph. Charlie Keller, another great player of the 1940s, was gone after the 1949 season.

It was sad to see them go but their words lingered.

COMPENSATE.

CONCENTRATE.

MOTIVATE.

PRACTICE.

I tried to absorb every ounce of knowledge these players could give. I knew I had talent. Did I have enough talent? If I didn't, I was willing to make up any shortcoming through a combination of compensation, concentration, motivation, and practice until I got where I intended to go.

Rizzuto had told me more than a couple of times, "God has a grand design for everyone and gave each of us sufficient ability to succeed in our chosen endeavor. The trick is to find your natural talents and then give it your all, your best, pay the price, and keep working at it."

Phil's talk about God's grand design echoed what I had heard from Brother Colombo more times than I could count. There could be no mistaking that in God's grand design Joe DiMaggio was destined to be a great baseball player. As much as one could compensate, concentrate, and practice, it was obvious that some people took the field with an enormous natural advantage.

I had talent, but not the "knock 'em dead" power of a Yogi Berra or the picture perfect swing of a DiMaggio. If I wanted to play baseball, I had to add value to the natural talent that had been given to me. I told myself, 'it's not so much the talent you're born with, it's how you use it.' Thoughts like that kept me going. At age fifteen, it never crossed my mind that my talents lay elsewhere. For me, there was only baseball.

16

Yogi and Mickey

The batboy's duties didn't end with the last out. As soon as the game was over, I was back in the clubhouse helping Pete Sheehy and Pete Previte pick up uniforms, shine shoes, do the laundry, sweep, and get the place in shape for the next day's game.

One great advantage of being in the Yankee clubhouse was tuning in on the conversations of baseball's greatest players. This opportunity to eavesdrop rarely presented itself in the visitor's clubhouse because the Red Sox or Indians or Senators were usually hurrying toward their next destination – a hotel in midtown Manhattan or a train at Grand Central Station. But the Yankees, who lived in New York City or New Jersey or some other place nearby, took time to unwind and would shoot the breeze over a beer or a Coke.

Sheehy often gave me the job of shining shoes and cleaning spikes. I didn't mind this assignment because I could stay in the same spot for about twenty minutes, which provided ample opportunity to pick up on a good conversation.

Not long after opening day in 1951, as I was digging the dried mud from cleats with a butter knife and applying saddle soap to the leather, I overheard Bill Dickey, the Yankee batting coach, hold forth on his theory of great hitters to Phil Rizzuto,

Yogi Berra, and a few others. Dickey was a shy man, but every once in a while this Hall of Fame catcher would go off on a jag about a subject that meant a great deal to him.

"I've been studying hitting and hitters for at least twenty years," said Dickey, "and I swear to you, you can't make a great hitter. Great hitters are born and all you can do as a trainer is sharpen their skills and maybe help refine certain aspects of their hitting style."

Dickey was in a position to know. He had worn the pin-stripes with Ruth and Gehrig and appeared with both of them in a famous photograph of the 1927 World Champions – still considered by many to be the best team that ever played the game. Until Yogi Berra came along, Dickey was the Yankees' all-time great catcher with a lifetime batting average of .313 and more than 200 home runs. In time, Dickey would be instru-mental in helping Yogi surpass the records he had established.

"I agree completely," said Yogi. "I never studied hitting, never even thought about it. I just played baseball with my friends from the neighborhood, played for my grammar school, my high school, and then the pros. I don't think much when I'm up at bat and never second guess what the pitcher will throw. You can teach a good hitter how to be better, but you can't teach a hitter to be good."

When Yogi said this, the small crowd that had gathered had a good laugh. Yogi's words often had this effect on the other players. As things started to break up, Rizzuto must've noticed the perplexed look on my face. He grabbed my shoulder and said with a smile, "Joseph, pay attention to Yogi. He is the epitome of a natural hitter – when he talks he makes a great deal of sense. Some day people are going to learn to take Yogi seriously."

"I agree with you, Phil. I just don't know why the guys think it's such a joke."

"Just the way he says it, Joe. I used to laugh too. But Yogi's words will come back to you a couple days later, and then you realize how right he is about a lot of things."

As Rizzuto walked away, I noted that Yogi didn't respond to the laughter; he wasn't hurt by it, and he didn't seem to get angry about it either. I had heard that Yogi took a lot of abuse from his teammates when he first played for the Yankees. He was a simple, unsophisticated kid. The son of Italian immigrants, it seemed as if English was a second language for him. His stocky build and big ears just didn't fit the All-American, good looking, Yankee image. But Yogi was always Yogi. He made no apologies for himself and didn't feel that he had to change to live up to other people's expectations. He was famous for reading the comics, and the latest editions of Casper the Friendly Ghost and Little Lulu were on display in his locker. Ironically, on road trips Yogi roomed with Doc Brown, the third baseman who was studying to be a cardiologist. They seemed to get along just fine.

His opponents and teammates were beginning to respect him as a great ballplayer, though. In 1950, he hit .322 and belted 28 homers and knocked in 128 runs. In 1951, he hit 27 home runs. As a player, he had arrived. It would be a while still before people would learn to pay attention to what he was saying. Little did anyone know in 1951 that Yogi would someday be quoted authoritatively by U.S. Presidents and championship coaches.

After the next day's game, as I was helping Sheehy clean up, Billy Martin and Yogi were the only players left in the clubhouse. Never to let an opportunity pass, I went over to Yogi's locker.

"Yogi, I couldn't help but overhear what you were saying yesterday about some people being naturally good hitters. Could you explain a little bit more about your philosophy of hitting?"

"Sure Joe. But I really don't have a philosophy of hitting. It's just either you have it or you don't. Either you are a natural or you will struggle. There are two kinds of baseball hitters. Those that hit good and those that are good hitters."

"What exactly do you mean by that?" I asked.

"Let me put it to you like this. Those that hit good are the players who have worked at it very hard and have improved their skills until they're very good at playing. On the other hand, the natural, the good hitter, starts above average and just improves his skills until he becomes excellent at what he does. Joe DiMaggio is a good hitter, Ted Williams is a good hitter. Oh, and that new kid, Mickey Mantle, he's a good hitter. Other players work hard at it and become players who hit good. Players who hit good will bat .275, .280. Good hitters will bat .310 or .320."

"I see what you mean, Yogi. Thanks a lot," I said.

Yogi's comment about "that new kid" Mantle struck a chord. No one could say enough about him. Mel Allen, who broadcast the spring training games from Florida said time and again that he had never seen a youngster like Mickey Mantle. Mel would announce that Mantle had cracked another thunderous home run, 440 or 450 feet, dubbing his shots a "White Owl Wallop" or a "Ballantine Blast" in deference to the particular Yankee sponsor of that portion of the broadcast. When the Yankees came back from Florida, a lot of the talk was about

Mantle's power and his ability to hit the ball farther than anyone could remember.

Mantle was only nineteen when he came up in 1951, but when I first saw him, he had the physique of a mature man, 23 or 24. In the '50s, the Yankee uniform was baggy by today's standards. Somehow Mantle made it look like it was tailor-made for him. His arms, his shoulders, and his neck were massive. He had the bulk of a weight lifter, but he had long, flexible muscles in his arms, the kind that DiMaggio and Williams had, the kind that seem essential for an exceptional hitter. And, amazingly, Mantle could hit from either side of the plate.

On opening day, the players couldn't wait to see Mantle take batting practice in Yankee Stadium. They had seen him knock the ball out of the park in Florida, but were anxious to see him hit his tape measure jobs inside Yankee Stadium for the first time. The entire bench cleared and the team gathered around the batting cage. While the pitching coach Jim Turner hurled the ball over the plate, Mantle, batting right handed, catapulted the ball into the left center field bleachers with ease. Some of the shots traveled more than 450 feet. The players, including DiMaggio, Berra, and Bauer – the power hitters – stood there in muted awe as he connected pitch after pitch after pitch. Although every player was supposed to take ten swings, nobody asked Mantle to leave after he had taken more then twenty cuts at the ball.

Feeling that he may have overstayed, he finally started to walk out of the batting cage. Rizzuto physically restrained him.

"Go back and hit some from the left side. This is something we want to see," Rizzuto said.

Although the left-handed drives didn't travel quite as far,

Mantle belted eight of ten pitches into the right field seats. I thought to myself, "If he can field like DiMaggio and hit like this, he'll be the greatest player that ever lived."

When it was over, a crowd gathered around him. But his face turned flush and he tried to wave them off. He couldn't take the attention. The boy wonder was painfully shy and modest.

About a week after my conversation with Yogi about great hitters, I was struck by the look of awe on Casey Stengel's face when he saw Mantle coming out of the shower with a towel draped around his waist. Casey said something like, "O my God! Your forearms are wider than my legs. What do you they feed you in Oklahoma?"

He mumbled something about eating lots of potatoes.

"If I had your muscles when I was playing baseball," said Casey, "I'd hit the ball out of the park every time. How'd you get those muscles, Mickey."

"Playing football and picking potatoes mostly, sir," he said.

Whenever you saw Casey, Billy Martin wasn't far behind. Right away, he tuned in on the conversation. "Yeah, I got my muscles from doing a lot of boxing. That really builds up the arms and the upper part of the body," said Billy, as he adopted a pose and flexed his muscles.

A small crowd gathered but no one but me noticed Billy's explanation of how he got his muscles. Mantle was the center of attention, a natural phenomenon from some never-heard-of place called Commerce, Oklahoma. Without opening his mouth, he would draw a crowd of admirers who would hang on every word he had to say. Billy, who actually had a lot more to say, was obviously one of those who'd have to work twice as hard for a fraction of the attention. Applying Yogi's philosophy, Mantle was a good hitter, Billy was someone who could learn to hit good.

Although nearly everyone considered Mantle the heir apparent to DiMaggio in center field, he had some competition. Jackie Jensen was another natural athlete. Like Mantle, he played football, had a massive physique, and was a long ball hitter. A lively competition developed between the two.

Since Joe Di rarely went to center field during batting and fielding practice in 1951, it was common to see both Mantle and Jensen shagging balls on DiMaggio's turf at the same time. The local sportswriters, sensing a story that would generate a lot of excitement, and certain that Joe Di would retire in 1951, played up the rivalry for all it was worth and a whole lot more.

So, it came as a shock when it was announced during the season that Mantle would be sent back to the minor leagues. The reporters wasted no time in writing obituaries for his brief career in New York.

On a quiet Saturday morning, with the team on the road, only Big Pete, Little Pete, Ralph, and I were in the clubhouse as Mantle gathered his personal effects and placed them slowly in his duffel bag. We all felt terrible for him. Mickey was trying to hold in his emotions, but he was close to tears.

Ralph said, "Don't worry Mickey, we'll see you back here – probably before the end of the year."

"Count on it, Ralph. I'll be back."

"How come Casey called you in the office, Mick?" Sheehy asked.

"Casey told me not to worry. Said I wasn't being sent down because I wasn't good. He said it was his decision to send me back to the minors 'cause he didn't want me to get rusty on the bench not playing everyday. Casey said that if DiMaggio doesn't come back in 1952, I'm the starting center fielder. Still in all, even though I know this is good for me, I'm going to miss being with the team and I'll miss Billy and Whitey and all the guys."

"If Casey said that, you can count on it," Sheehy said.

Once in a generation appears a baseball player whose talent seems to come from another world. Joe Di had been such a player, and it was obvious from the first day he took the field that Mantle was another. It seemed only right and natural that someone as talented as Mickey would be the successor to DiMaggio in the Yankee dynasty.

Casey, the wise and wily Ol' Perfesser, who, it seemed, had been around longer than everybody else put together, knew what he had in Mickey Mantle. He wasn't about to let this extraordinary resource get away from him for very long. Mickey was the engine that would pull the Yankees to future glory. Casey saw that from the beginning. As Casey promised, Mickey's tenure in the minors was brief indeed.

17

The Wise Men

"B-E-E-A-H-H H-E-E-A-H-H."
"S-O-O-O-D-A-H."
"H-O-T D-O-G-G-G-S."
"P-E-E-E-N-U-T-S."
"P-O-P K-A-W-N-N."

That's the ballpark's background music, sung by the vendors as they hawk their goods up and down the stadium's aisles. It's so constant and reliable that you never even think about it... never, that is, until it stops.

In all my years at Yankee Stadium the music stopped but once. Before the start of a night game, it was as if someone pulled the plug on a record player...BEAH H..., HOT D..., SOOOD..., PEEEN..., POPKAAA.... The sounds just trailed away.

As I stood on the top step of the dugout moments before the National Anthem was to be sung, I noticed the change in decibel level and scanned the stands behind home plate. All eyes were focused on someone in the box seats. President Truman or Governor Dewey wouldn't have generated this much interest. 'Who could it be?' I asked myself.

Then I saw her. A gorgeous, blonde beauty, whose every bouncing step down the aisle sent a little shudder of excitement through the crowd. 'So' I whispered, 'it's true after all.'

A rumor had made its way quietly through the Yankee club-house that Joe DiMaggio, the baseball legend, was dating a young Hollywood starlet named Marilyn Monroe. No one believed it even though the story had made its way into "The Confidential," the 1950s equivalent of the National Enquirer. The idea that the sub-dued, Joe Di, the great American baseball hero, could be coupled, in public, with this vivacious idol of the American cinema was... a shocker.

But there she was – in the box seats reserved for the Yankee owner, Dan Topping. Even at 100 feet, she was...if not the most beautiful woman that I had ever seen, certainly the most diverting.

"Hey Joe," I heard from somewhere behind me, but I couldn't take my eyes off her.

"Hey Joe the batboy, get your head in the game," said Frank Crosetti with a big grin.

I turned around. Frank was pointing toward the exit to the clubhouse.

"Pete Sheehy needs a hand. He asked for you."

I looked at Frank, shrugged and smiled. He understood, but his look said 'we're here to play baseball, not watch Marilyn Monroe.' I backed slowly into the exit, gazing into the stands as long as I could.

It was pretty hard to distract Frank Crosetti. Marilyn Monroe did little more than bring a smile to his craggy face. Not that Crosetti was that old – I don't think he was much older than Joe Di. But Crosetti probably felt that Marilyn Monroe was a dis-traction from the more important things in life. He would never say that to Joe Di. Nobody would dare.

But where Crosetti may have hesitated to reproach Joe Di, he didn't hesitate to dispense advice to the younger players – or, for that matter, to me. Crosetti was a coach first and last. He never took his mind off winning ball games. Toward that end, he lent an enormous amount of encouragement and advice to the younger players while demanding that they "always keep their head in the game." That's what a coach is supposed to do.

Between 1949 and 1953, the Yankees won five consecutive World Series. No team has done that before or since. Although there's no shortage of theories about the secret of their success – from the genius of Casey Stengel to the talent of their pitchers, from the experience of DiMaggio to the power of Mantle – not enough attention has been paid to the Yankees' extraordinary coaching staff of that era.

Besides Crosetti, the Yankees had a gifted pitching coach in Jim Turner and a brilliant batting coach in Bill Dickey.

Crosetti combined a strict code – swearing was strictly prohibited in his presence – with shrewdness, discipline, and an overwhelming desire to win.

He was always concerned with keeping players focused. He seemed to feel that distractions, on and off the field, made for sloppy play and lost ball games. Crosetti was a deeply religious, family man, which meant that he kept most of life's normal distractions at a distance. But he tried to keep the younger players from going astray – both on and off the field.

Besides his duties as the third base coach, Crosetti also managed the infield. This is where his shrewdness and morality came together. He played to win, capitalized on every advantage, but he also taught his players that there was a right and wrong way to do it. Believing that a team's infield was the key to a successful defense, Crosetti spent many early-morning hours disciplining the infield players.

Rizzuto was a sensational shortstop and Doc Brown played a solid third base. With these two as his foundation, Crosetti took the less experienced players like Gil McDougald, Billy Martin, and Jerry Coleman and drilled them tirelessly, hitting ball after ball with the long, thin fungo bat. All the time he did this, he was talking to them about positioning, timing, and how to make the double play. They practiced until they had choreographed their moves to an impossible degree of perfection.

Rizzuto obviously occupied a special place in Crosetti's heart. Not only was Phil a great defensive player, he gave his complete support to Frank by encouraging the younger players to do it "Crow's" way. Phil also continued the Yankee tradition of great Italian shortstops. Frank held the position before Phil, playing for the Yankees from 1932 to 1948. Before Crosetti, during the era of Ruth and Gehrig, shortstop was played by Tony Lazzeri.

If Frank was the heart of the Yankee infield, then Jim Turner was the guiding intelligence behind the Yankees' pitching success. A gentle, soft-spoken man, Turner himself had a brief pitching career with the Yankees during the war years 1942-45. Nicknamed the Milkman, Turner excelled as a coach in a way he never did as a player. His major league totals show only 69 wins against 60 losses. His pitching staff excelled though, and the Yankee pitchers under his tutelage dominated baseball for years. Although the Yankees of that era were known as the Bronx Bombers for obvious reasons, the excellence of the pitching staff was sometimes overlooked. By 1951 though, everyone knew the Yankees' pitching complemented their hitting prowess. How could anyone have missed that in the 1950 World Series, Lopat, Reynolds, Ford, and Raschi allowed just five runs in four games (not all of them earned) as the Yankees swept the World Series from the Phillies?

Turner spent his coaching career studying the hitters and pitchers on every team the Yankees played. He knew the opposition inside out. Perhaps his greatest talent was his ability to develop strong relationships with his pitchers. He bonded to them like a good father to his sons and, inevitably, one of his sons sat next to him during a game discussing the opposing pitcher's stuff and the hitter's strengths and weaknesses. He earned their admiration and respect and I think each of them went the extra mile for him.

As much as Turner thought you could become a winner by understanding the strengths and weaknesses of your opponents, he also believed that most losing pitchers were done in by fatigue, not bad pitching. Turner had a simple remedy for this: "Run, Run, Run."

He used to say, "Your legs will go long before your arm does." Time and again, Jim told this to the younger players like Whitey Ford and Frank Shea. The senior members – Raschi, Lopat, Reynolds – knew it by heart.

Turner's strategy to improve conditioning was quite simple. Build up your legs. Because a pitcher expends so much energy pushing off the mound, his legs are subject to enormous stresses. Turner wanted to keep those legs strong. He also recognized, well ahead of his time, that running was the key to cardiovascular fitness.

But Turner also knew that running is boring. So he devised a method to liven it up – having his pitchers run from left to right field while he hit them long drives. At first, the pitchers came up short. But after a week or two of practice, the pitchers were making easy catches in right field and were actually beginning to like the drill. This routine was not just for the rookies – Turner had the veterans like Reynolds and Lopat doing the same thing.

After about a month of this practice, the pitchers obviously had more staying power. Instead of being worn out by the fifth or sixth inning, they were going seven, eight, or nine innings. The joke was that Turner was losing jobs for the relief pitchers.

Turner felt so strongly about running that he refused to allow the team to buy a golf cart to bring in a pitcher from the bullpen. Although the Yankees were behind the times – most of the major league teams drove their pitchers to the mound – Jim believed that even those few extra steps were an added advantage for his pitchers that shouldn't be passed up.

If Crosetti represented heart and Turner intelligence, then Bill Dickey symbolized the pride of the Yankee tradition. If you were good enough to be a Yankee, then you had something to live up to – to be your personal best, not for yourself, but for the tradition of greatness that was the Yankees.

Dickey believed that Yankee greatness was grounded in their hitting prowess. His devotion to improving both individual and team hitting performance was nearly religious.

I often overheard him tell the younger players, "You are not carpenters using a hammer and a screwdriver and a drill. You are not doctors with scalpels and stethoscopes. You are baseball players and you have very little in the way of tools other than your own physical abilities and your major instrument, your bat. You bat is your livelihood. It's your best friend.

"Take Minnesota Fats," he went on, "it's reported that he doesn't go anywhere without his pool cue. He is constantly fingering the cue to know every facet of it, and that is what you should be doing with your bats.

"Look, you rookies must get comfortable with your bats. Your bat is an extension of your own body and you should be swinging it at all times. You should take it home with you. You should bring it in the backyard. In the clubhouse, swing the bat; in the dugout, have the bat in your hands. Just feel so comfortable with the baseball bat that it becomes part of your physical being, an appendage, another arm, so that when you get up at the plate, you don't even think about it."

Dickey's intense pride was never more evident than in the time he devoted to making Yogi Berra a first rate catcher. While Yogi was a naturally great hitter, after a couple of years with the team he was still not completely comfortable behind the plate. The veteran Yankee pitchers knew this and insisted on calling their own pitches. This is unusual. A good catcher usually tells a pitcher what to throw since he knows his pitcher's strengths and weaknesses and has a feel for the batter in the box. At the very least, there's a give-and-take between pitcher and catcher as they decide on the best pitch.

When Allie Reynolds or Eddie Lopat pitched, he regularly shook off Yogi's call if it wasn't the pitch he wanted – whether it was one finger for the fastball, two for the curve, or three for the slider. Neither Reynolds nor Lopat was about to let an insecure youngster make that decision for him.

Dickey, who, until Yogi Berra came along, had been the Yankee's greatest catcher, felt this was an insult to Yogi's pride – to Bill Dickey's pride – in fact, to any catcher's pride. Dickey worked with Yogi until he had pumped up his confidence to the point that Yogi grabbed Eddie Lopat one day and said, "I'm calling the pitches today." There was no argument. Yogi knew he could do it and, with Dickey's help, he had the confidence that he had what it takes to call the pitches.

The coaching staff was naturally overshadowed by Casey Stengel. But Crosetti, Turner, and Dickey never upstaged their manager. Instead, they set a quiet, supportive tone that other members of the team picked up on. There was no rancor or destructive competitiveness on the team. Instead, there was an unusual harmony. Like a good family, the Yankees loved to be with each together. If a family member was in trouble – in a slump, not playing up to potential, or making mistakes – more than likely, one of the coaches or an older player would talk to him, work with him, and try and get him on track. That's what helped the team. That's what made the Yankees great!

18

Grown up

In June 1951, Red Patterson, the Yankees road secretary told me to pack my bags. By the end of the month, I'd be riding the rails with the New York Yankees. From station stop to station stop, the journey would last seventeen days and cover half the country.

I was incredibly excited and just as anxious. I thanked Red but never let on what was troubling me.

It was a tradition for the Yankees to take selected members of the clubhouse staff, including the batboy, on one road trip each summer. This trip had been the highlight of Ralph's summers for a few years. But Ralph wouldn't be traveling with the team in 1951. He was the visiting clubhouse man and his job was in New York. That was the source of my anxiety.

I knew my mother would be reluctant to let me go if my brother wasn't there to keep an eye on me. I didn't know why though. After all, I was fifteen, I had finished my first year in high school, and I had been working at Yankee Stadium for two years. Moreover, I would be in good company. How could she say no. In a word...easy. She was a mother and I was her youngest child.

Knowing in advance that I would be invited to travel with the team at some point during the summer months, I tried for weeks to soften Mom up, dropping hints about how I looked forward to traveling with the team someday. She was too smart for that. She didn't say no, she just avoided the topic until I brought it out into the open.

She didn't have to wait long. The day that Red told me about the trip, I asked her flat out...and she answered, "No, no, no."

I begged. I pleaded. I cajoled. I wheedled. She was immovable.

"You're still a baby," she said.

"No I'm not. I can take care of myself. Can't you see. I'm grown up."

"You're not. You must wait one more year. That's that."

There was no point in seeking my father's intervention. When it came to big decisions, Mom called the shots and Dad went along for the ride.

A day or two after I got the news of the trip from Red, Phil Rizzuto called me over to his cubicle before the start of a game. He reached inside and pulled out an over-sized valise.

"Go home and pack, Joe," said Phil.

"You're unbelievable. You think of everything, don't you?"

"Seventeen days is a long time. You might want to change your shirt."

"I don't know if I'm going to make it Phil," I said, close to tears. "My mom's against the idea."

"Thinks you're not old enough? I can appreciate that. Say, how about telling her I'll keep an eye on you."

"I don't know if even that will cut it. When her mind is made up, it's hard to turn her around. I can't believe it. I've never been further away than New Jersey. This was my big chance to see some of the country. It's going to kill me."

"Well, we have a couple of weeks. We'll think of something."

"I hope you're right, Phil. But you don't know my mom."

I didn't let on to anyone, even to Phil, another source of disappointment. I knew this would be my last, best chance to talk to Joe DiMaggio. Everyone knew he would call it quits at the end of the '51 season. He was tired and worn. After every game, it took him a couple of hours just to regain enough strength to dress and go home. But now I'd be on the road for days, traveling from city to city by train, staying in the same hotel with the team. I was sure I'd have more opportunities to speak to Joe Di than I had had in the past two years.

When I got home and opened up my new suitcase from Phil, there was another surprise inside – $28 in singles, a gift from all the players and coaches, and a $20 check from Casey Stengel. Now I felt worse than ever.

If Mom was impressed by the Yankees' largesse, she didn't let on. She told me I could hold onto the suitcase until the next year. The money had to be returned. Her mind was set.

There was no way I was going to win this argument, I told myself. I could wait another twelve months for the trip, but I couldn't accept that I'd never again have the chance to travel with Joe DiMaggio. Just as I said that to myself, the phone rang. Ralph picked it up.

"Mom, it's for you. It's Phil Rizzuto."

"Sure, it's Phil Rizzuto," she answered with a laugh. "Who is it really? It's Aunt Nettie, right?"

"No, Mom. It's Phil. I'm not kidding."

"I got as near to Mom and the phone as I could, sitting on the edge of the couch while Mom picked up the receiver."

"O, hi Phil. It really is you," she sounded like a schoolgirl. My mother's face turned red. In all my years, it was the first time I had seen my mother blush.

"Okay, okay. He's just a little young. Uh-huh. Well...since you put it that way.... Well, it's very nice of you to say that. Yes, they are good boys."

Phil came through, promising Mom that I could room with him and that he'd keep an eye on me for the entire trip. Then he told her what an outstanding job she had done with both Ralph and me. He found her weak spot. Flattery overcame all objections.

The entire Carrieri household was soon involved in getting me ready for my big trip. Mom and Dad took me to the shopping center at 149th Street and Third Avenue in the Bronx. After visiting Hearn's department store, Vim's, DeVeeger's, and Alexander's, we came home with two shopping bags full of slacks, shirts, shoes, sneakers, socks, and a dinner jacket. (Ralph had warned me that when eating dinner in the hotels, "gentlemen" were required to wear appropriate attire.)

During our shopping spree, I picked up a road map of the forty-eight states. For the next week, in bed at night, I studied the distances and the towns in-between New York New York, Cleveland Ohio, Detroit Michigan, St. Louis Missouri, and Washington D.C.

My mom did her best to hide her anxieties, but they came out in little ways. She was obsessed with the notion that I might not eat properly or enough when I was beyond her care. At least twice a day for the next week, she warned me, "Joe, remember, don't be bashful. EAT!" Even my ever-reticent dad seemed a little concerned. He reminded me over and over again, "Joe, don't forget... *mangia, mangia.*"

Since my family didn't own a car in 1951, a few of our neighbors with wheels offered to drive me to Grand Central Station. I thanked them all and politely refused. This whole experience was as much a rite of passage for Mom and Dad as it was for me. I sensed how much they wanted it to be a family affair when they sent me off.

When the big day arrived, I hurried home after a Sunday afternoon game at Yankee Stadium so I could pick up my suitcase and the $48 the Yankees had given me. As I headed toward the door, suitcase in hand, my dad put his arm around my shoulder, pulled me close, and pushed a twenty dollar bill into my shirt pocket. "You never know..." he started. But I finished the sentence for him "...I might get hungry." He just laughed.

Ralph, Mom, Dad, and I boarded the IRT subway at 138th Street and Lincoln Avenue in the Bronx. In twenty minutes, we were at Grand Central Station at 42nd Street in Manhattan. As we approached Gate 16, there was excitement in the air. Several hundred Yankee fans had gathered to bid the team farewell. They were waving banners, asking for autographs, and calling the players by name as they passed through the gate. I felt giddy and light-headed.

We paused as the Yankees streamed through. Amid the jostling, I was able to introduce my parents to Gil McDougald, Billy Martin, Joe Collins, Johnny Mize, Hank Bauer, Gene Woodling, Whitey Ford, and Yogi Berra.

Finally, Ralph said, "Joe, time to go. Get on the train. You don't want to be left behind."

I kissed Mom, who was now teary-eyed, and shook Dad's hand. Ralph put his arm around me and walked me to the gate.

"Stay with the team," were his parting words.

"Don't worry. Don't worry. You're starting to sound like Mom. Everything will be fine."

I shook my brother's hand. "I'll see you in seventeen days."

I crossed the platform into the train, turned, and waved a final good-bye to the trio that had seen me so far, so well.

19

In his own words

Twenty-five players, Red Patterson, trainer Gus Mauch, Casey Stengel, and the three coaches, Bill Dickey, Jim Turner, and Frank Crosetti, occupied two Pullman cars in the center of the train. Also along for the trip were a half dozen or so reporters from the New York Times, the Daily News, the Daily Mirror, the Herald Tribune, and the Journal American.

As I boarded, Patterson was inside the door with a clipboard. "Joe, you're in Number 22," he told me as he checked off my name. I walked a short way down the narrow aisle and opened the door with the 22 on it. The room had a two-seater with a fold down bed. It also had its own sink, toilet, and chair.

Seconds later, someone knocked. I opened the door to find Billy Martin standing outside. "Joe, don't get lost. Phil wants you to check in with him as soon as you get settled."

"Sure thing," I answered.

Red had told me that it would take about twelve hours to get to Cleveland. We were due to arrive at nine in the morning.

No sooner had I thrown my suitcase on the bed than the train lurched forward. Soon my compartment started to vibrate and the wheels began to sing, "minimanush minimanush minimanush." I said to myself, half-laughing "Oh no. I'll never get to sleep tonight." I was right on top of the wheels.

I left the compartment and followed the crowd to the dining car. Most of the team was inside. As I walked in, I was greeted with, "Hey Joe, glad you could make it. Pull up a chair." And then Yogi chipped in, "Hey Joe, did they give you the wheels?"

"How'd you know?"

Mickey Mantle yelled, "Don't feel bad. You got the front wheels, I got the back."

This was my introduction to the pecking order on the Yankees. While Joe DiMaggio and Allie Reynolds were nestled snugly in the center of the car, the scrubinis, rookies, not-so-famous reporters, and the Yankee batboy were positioned right above the train wheels – the noisiest, most uncomfortable part of the train.

I didn't mind at all.

I sat down in the dining car with Rizzuto, Berra, and Jerry Coleman. Yogi told me, "Don't be shy." The players were famous for chowing down on these trips because the Yankee management picked up the tab. Almost to a man, the Yankees were steak eaters. Yogi ordered a well-done sirloin, mashed potatoes, and peas and carrots, and an iced tea. Coleman was having his medium-well with a baked potato, a tossed salad and a Coke. When the waiter looked at me, I said, "I'll take the same."

Joe Di was sitting at the next table with Frank Crosetti, Vic Raschi, and Billy Martin. Joe dug into a rare steak, a baked potato saturated with butter, and a lettuce and tomato salad topped with olives. Like a surgeon, he cut away the fat from his steak. He washed it all down with coffee. You rarely saw Joe drinking a beer, but he was a very heavy coffee drinker.

I had heard the players rave about the train food. Now I knew why. My steak was tender, and my first meal memorably delicious.

Everyone ordered the deep dish apple pie for dessert. I noticed that Mickey Mantle and Billy Martin were on their second round of pie ala mode by the time I ordered mine.

Coleman sat next to Phil so they could talk shop as they ate dinner. Phil had at least five more years to play, but when Phil was injured, Coleman was the substitute.

Phil enjoyed the audience and Coleman absorbed everything Phil had to say.

"When Eddie Lopat's pitching," said Phil, "I play a step or two closer to third base with a right-handed hitter. Because Eddie throws the slow stuff, hitters get out in front of the pitch and tend to pull the ball."

"When Allie Reynolds is pitching," said Phil, I play a step or two closer to second. Allie's a fast ball pitcher, so the ball's coming straight off the bat.

"When Vic Raschi is on the mound," Phil continued, "I play somewhere in between the two positions.

"If a fast left-handed batter is up, I play a step or two in so I can nip him at first. If someone like Ted Williams is up, I play a step or two back, giving me more of a chance to field his hard one hoppers."

Phil was painting mental pictures, describing for Coleman how to execute the double play, how to time his jump when he threw the ball, and how to avoid the high spikes when a runner made the hard slide into second. Phil also shared his defensive strategy on some of the best hitters in the league such as Dom DiMaggio, Joe's brother in Boston, and Al Rosen.

As always, Joe Di's shadow, aka Billy Martin, was at the great one's elbow. I think Billy hoped that some of Joe Di's greatness would rub off on him. Billy was peppering Joe with questions. Joe Di was not known to linger and socialize, but this was an unusual night.

"What do you look for from Bob Feller?" Billy asked Joe about the great Cleveland pitcher.

"Bob Feller is so effective because he not only has a hopping fast ball, he also has an exceptionally sharp breaking curve," said Joe.

"Billy, always be prepared to swing at a three and one pitch," Joe offered. "That may be the difference between a good hitter and a great hitter.

"Most players with a three and one count are hoping for the walk. They are hesitant to take a swing on a close pitch for fear that they may be criticized by the manager or the coaches. But let me tell you one thing, the pitcher is as worried about throwing a bad pitch as you are about swinging at one. He doesn't want to walk the batter and get in trouble. So I have learned through the years that the pitcher on a three and one usually lets off on his fast ball or his curve ball to control his pitch and throw the strike. That's the batter's edge. Be ready to swing because you'll never get a better pitch than a three and one."

It was unusual for Joe Di to talk like this. In my two years with the team, I had never heard anything like this from the Yankee Clipper. I could tell that everyone in the car felt the same way. The dining car became unusually quiet and everyone was listening in. Phil and Jerry stopped talking to hear what Joe had to say.

"Billy," Joe continued, "life is a risk and when you play baseball you have to take risks. As a center fielder, I could have played the line drive on the short hop for a single. That would have been playing it safe. Instead, I always went the extra inch to try to catch it on a fly. Sure, you might miss it and be charged with an error, but that is what separates the major league ball-player from the minor league ballplayer – the ability to take the risk and make the catch."

"The same thing applies on the base pads. Many a time I could have stopped at first base with a single. Instead, I stretched many singles into doubles when I thought the out-fielder was not expecting me to make the run for second base. Sure, I could have been thrown out at second and wasted the hit, but many times I scored from second on a single and that is why I took the risk in the first place. You're still young, Billy. You have many good years ahead of you. Don't always play it safe. When you see an opportunity, take the risk, stretch a double into a triple, steal second base when your opponent least expects it. Go for that fly ball that might normally drop between the outfielder and infielder. What do you have to lose if you give it your all and dive after it and miss it. It will only be a single, but if you catch it, it could save the game.

"To us men of autumn, it is still a game. But I am afraid it is starting to become a business, and when that happens, all of the fun will be out of it. I hope that doesn't happen real soon."

By this time, it was so quiet that not a dish rattled. Even the waiters had stopped to listen to Joe's words. Joe, who suddenly realized that he had a rapt audience, withdrew into his normal, quiet self.

The train blew its whistle, and Joe said, "I've done a lot of talking tonight. I guess I'll turn in."

He got up and headed for the door. Only Billy followed him out.

After a minute or so, the place came back to life. I was very excited. "Did you ever hear Joe talk like that, Phil?" I asked.

"It's a rarity. I think Billy can get him to talk like very few can."

Defining DiMaggio was a little like defining God. You could describe his attributes, but the essence was a lot harder to discover. I knew Joe had remarkable courage, great determination, natural ability. I knew he played baseball for baseball's sake – for the love of the game first and foremost. And now I knew in his own words, that to win he was willing to take extraordinary risks and to go the extra mile.

The book on Joe Di was not closed after all. The story was developing. Although I had a lot more to learn, I had a feeling of synchronicity about the trip – a sense that this was the right time and place for me to uncover the secret to Joe's success and to get to know him in a way that I never could in the Yankee clubhouse. It was a great beginning to my journey.

20

Casey

After DiMaggio's departure, the festive atmosphere quickly returned to the dining car. As soon as the dishes were cleared, some players asked the conductor to bring on the playing cards. For the next couple of hours, the car was transformed into a gambling parlor. Although a few guys played hearts and love, the real thing was blackjack, poker, and gin rummy. Through the hazy cigarette smoke and above the clinking beer bottles, the shouts of "hit me," "ya in," "I'll raise ya" and "whataya got" filled the car. Rizzuto and I joined a poker game, playing a quarter a hand. Once the pot was as high as $5, but my sixty-eight-dollar endowment was never in jeopardy.

Nobody lost any real money and it was never the object of our entertainment. Poker and gin rummy were just a way for the players to pass the time while they shared their obsession. Baseball was the common denominator, the thread that pulled us all together. We were a brotherhood of ballplayers, bonded in some mystical, incomprehensible fashion. Of a single mind, each of us loved baseball as richly and fully as life itself.

I was the novice, but I was welcome and I felt their love, not just for the game but for each other. Each person was equally accepted. And as Billy tried to convince Mickey that he could bat .400 if he learned to bunt and Phil talked of double-play balls, the "old timer" Bill Dickey pontificated on his favorite subject.

"There's two types of hitters," Dickey said. "The first anticipates what the pitcher will throw, whether it's a fast ball or slow curve. The second type doesn't think about the next pitch... because he's ready, no matter what's thrown to him."

Yogi said, "I never guess what the pitcher is about to throw because I leave my mind a complete blank. That way I can't be fooled."

"Yogi, your mind is always blank, so it really doesn't make any difference," said Hank Bauer. The chorus of laughter included Yogi, who enjoyed the joke as well as anyone.

In the midst of all this, Casey Stengel got up and ambled toward the door. He stopped, turned and looked at Yogi and said, "Yogi, I never saw anyone swing at such bad balls in all my life. You'll hit a ball two feet over your head or two inches off the ground. If you ever waited to just swing at strikes, you would be a .400 hitter." Casey turned and started for the door.

Yogi turned a little red in the face. Unintentionally, Casey had killed the mood. The dining car was suddenly very quiet. There had been an edge to Casey's words, and it sounded like he was putting Yogi down. Casey sensed it right away. He caught himself before he was out the door, turned around, pointed at Yogi and shouted, "But you can get away with it. You're a natural. Don't change your style for anybody, not even me, because if you did, you wouldn't be Yogi."

Now, Yogi was smiling as Casey made his exit. The games resumed, and the Yankees' catcher, with a big grin on his face, called "gin rummy."

Casey wasn't dealt in to any of the card games, but he was

in and out of the car all evening long. Like a watchful parent, he seemed to want his boys to have fun; but at the same time, he didn't want things to get out of hand. With the exception of his remark to Yogi, he had a way of making his presence felt without really intruding.

Somewhere between eleven and midnight, the players started drifting back to their rooms.

"Why don't you do like me and turn in, Joe," Rizzuto said around midnight. "You know we have a game to play tomorrow and there'll be no time to catch a nap when we get to the hotel."

Although I was wide awake and enjoying myself, the last thing I wanted to do was argue with my patron. I followed Rizzuto out of the car.

As I headed toward Compartment 22, I noticed that the door to Joe Di's room was open. He was lying on his bed. Billy, who had been in and out of the dining car, was wrapped in a blanket, lying at DiMaggio's feet. They were chatting like the best of friends. Stranger sights I have rarely seen. I wished I knew Billy's secret.

When I opened the door to Compartment 22, I lay down without changing my clothes. My eyes were wide open. The wheels sang "minimanush, minimanush, minimanush," the train whistle blew at every crossing and, with my arms folded beneath my head, I stared out the window at the contrast of light and dark as we hurtled through town and country.

I was too excited to sleep. I could hardly believe that I was here with the Yankees on the most important trip of my life. With each passing mile, the train carried me further away from my old, familiar world. I felt as if I was hurrying toward a future that was new, exciting and beyond anything I could have ever imagined on my tenement stoop in the South Bronx.

It seemed my eyes never closed. I drifted off to a peaceful place between sleep and wakefulness, noticing every station stop and crossing signal through a hazy cloud. I remembered Joe Di's voice through the rhythmic sound of the wheels, "Don't always play it safe.... When you see an opportunity, take the risk.... What do you have to lose if you give it your all?..."

When the porter knocked on my door at seven-thirty, it seemed like I had never slept. I jumped up, threw water on my face, and joined the players again in the dining car for coffee and rolls. We were due in Cleveland Station in ninety minutes.

Outside the station, a bus was waiting for us. It was less than a ten minute ride to the Wade Park Manor, a grand old hotel in downtown Cleveland. Valise in hand, I followed Rizzuto through the lobby where a small crowd of autograph-seekers had gathered to meet the team.

They mobbed Joe Di, who was trying to pass through as inconspicuously as possible. That was impossible.

Red Patterson assigned rooms when we got to the hotel and Rizzuto and I took the elevator to the 18th floor. The door to Room 1805 opened to a huge, luxurious suite with twin beds, a sofa, club chair, several dressers, night tables, and a television.

Rizzuto paid for the television out of his own pocket. In 1951, it was not yet part of the standard hotel room package, but Rizzuto loved old movies, especially mysteries. He also loved the fights. It was the era of great Italian boxers, from the Rocky's (Graziano and Marciano) to Jake LaMotta, and Rizzuto never missed the blow by blow provided by Bill Corum at the Friday night fights.

The Yankees and Indians had a game the same afternoon,

so we no sooner unpacked and showered than we were leaving for Cleveland Stadium. The bus that brought us to the hotel was waiting to drive us the short hop to the ballpark.

I was almost on the bus when Rizzuto called from behind me. I turned and saw him getting into a taxi. He motioned for me to follow. A few of the players were taking cabs, including Joe Di. When I jumped in the taxi next to Phil, he told me he hated buses and avoided them whenever he could.

When we arrived at Cleveland Municipal Stadium, the team bus was already there. When Phil and I stepped out of the cab, Frank Crosetti was over me like a big blanket.

"Where were you Joe? We were starting to worry. We saw you getting on the bus and then we didn't see you no more. Casey wants you. On the double."

I couldn't get a word in if I tried and Crosetti cut off Rizzuto's explanation. I hurried off to find the Yankee manager.

When I knocked on the half-opened door to his office in the visiting clubhouse, I was more than a little nervous.

"Come on in," yelled Casey.

"Joe," he said with a smile on his face, "if you get lost one more time, we are going to put a lasso around your neck and just tie it to one of the players."

I started to relax.

"Seriously, Joe, when you are on the road with me and the players, you have become part of my family and I feel responsible. So please let us know where you are going and who you are going with."

"Sorry Casey. I was with Phil. But it won't happen again," I promised.

"Okay, son, but stay with the team. Now, let's get to work."

Twice in two days, I got a glimpse of the Old Professor in action. For someone who could seem so out of touch, he was on top of everything – including the whereabouts of his batboy.

The Yankees lost the first game of their series with the Indians. After the game, Casey put out the word that he was holding a manager's meeting – team members only. The press never made its way past the locker room door. When the visiting clubhouse man left, I thought I should probably go too. But no one said a word, so I stayed right where I was.

Casey Stengel spoke for over an hour. His total recall and analysis of the play-by-play was amazing. At the same time, his presentation was unique. He spoke in paragraphs rather than sentences, and although his syntax and grammar were unorthodox, he was understood clearly by all.

"Look, we are here to do one thing. We are here to win. Nobody is better than you. We got power – DiMag. We got speed – Mantle. We got the best bunter in the league – Rizzuto. We got the big cat – Mize. And we got the best pitching staff in both leagues – Raschi, Reynolds, Lopat, and Ford. Why, our second string players are better than most of their first. We got one of the best catchers in baseball sitting on the bench – Charlie Silvera. Why, we even have the best batboy – young Joe Carrieri."

He could've knocked me over with the whiff of a bat. In that moment of recognition, Casey not only welcomed me to the family, he made me feel that I was an important part of it. In my heart, I knew I would've done anything for the guy.

After Casey finished stroking his players, he applied the stick.

"Look, I've got twenty-five players and only nine positions.

Everybody wants to play and I have to make a decision about who's going to play and who's going to sit the bench. I don't want to make that decision, so you are going to make it for me. I am going to two-platoon you and I'm going to switch players. Sometimes Mize will play first base, sometimes Collins. At second, it's Martin or Coleman; at third base, I'll two-platoon Johnson and Brown. At short, Rizzuto, as long as your arm holds out, that is your job. Catching will be Yogi and when I rest him, Silvera is behind the plate. In right field, Bauer and Mapes will play. DiMaggio has center field and when he is out Mantle plays. Woodling is in left field and when he's out Jensen is in.

"I believe in the two-platoon system. One, it keeps you players on your toes; two, it gives you a needed rest; three, we work as a team, not a bunch of individuals; and four, it's the right thing to do. If you go four for four and hit two home runs, don't be surprised if you play every day. By the same token, if you go into a slump, why aggravate the situation. Let's give another guy a chance."

Casey went on, "Look, I know you guys are young and you want to go out at night and have a few beers. I was your age once and I used to do those things. I know you are going to do them. But now I am the manager. And you can't do them when lights go out at 10 p.m. and you have to be in your room. I don't want to catch anyone in the hotel lobby at 3 o'clock in the morning telling me he was mailing a letter to his sick grandmother."

The room cracked in laughter. Joe Page's explanation of his late night forays, though more than a year old, was now the stuff of Yankee legend.

"I have the fullest faith in your integrity that you will abide by our curfews and you will be in your room every night at ten, unless of course there is a night game."

Casey closed with his own inimitable logic.

"I know I can trust you and that is why we have retained the services of two private investigators. We retained the investigators so that I won't be disappointed in any of you breaking the rules."

When Casey finally finished and walked out of the gathering, Crosetti and the other coaches remained behind for another minute. The place was still quiet as Crosetti closed with a short oration.

"You want to know why the Yankees are great? Follow the man who just walked through that door."

For Crosetti, words mattered, and he spoke right to the heart of the issue. The Yankees of the early 1950s were a team that loved to be together. They joked, laughed, sang, and drank like one big partying family. But the guiding light was the father, who disciplined and directed his team with one purpose in mind. Casey hated to lose and he hated being second best. And although many of the players seemed mystified by Casey's monologues, if not by his coaching methods, Crosetti understood him completely because they both wanted the same thing. They both cared first and foremost about winning. And whether it took platooning the veterans with the younger players, soft-soaping Yogi Berra after he had insulted him, playing dad to the new guys, or acting the fool to keep his opponents off-balance, Casey was willing to do whatever was necessary so that, come October, the Yankees would be standing in the winner's circle.

Beginning that first day in Cleveland, I got in the habit of sending postcards to Mom, Dad, and Ralph. Invariably, the postcard was a picture of the hotel where the Yankees were staying. I knew Mom liked to see the postmarks from faraway places. Usually, I just told them about the food, the hotel, and the guys. What I didn't need to say was that I was having the time of my life with the greatest bunch of guys I could imagine.

I had left the safe, secure world of my South Bronx neighborhood, a boy becoming a man. For me and the Yankees, we weren't just having fun. Because this family had a kind, but strict father, it had a direction and purpose that any other team would have envied. For if we were willing to listen to Casey, accept his disciplines, and see it his way, we were bound to remain the Champions of the World.

21

Man of autumn

With the exception of Joe DiMaggio, most of the players I spoke to had a ready answer to my question about the meaning of success. Many responded from the gut, as if they knew without thinking about it what contributed most to their personal success. For Jackie Robinson it was persistence, for Joe Page – concentration, for Yogi Berra – sheer natural talent. Phil Rizzuto tried twice as hard because he was half the size of the big, strong guys.

From time to time, I reminded myself of Jackie Robinson's words as I tried to get the final word on the subject from the grand old man of autumn, Joe DiMaggio. But persistence alone was not enough. I needed a little luck.

There were many barriers around Joe DiMaggio. Reticent, reclusive, reserved. Those were the words that popped into my head when I thought of him. By accident or design, he kept himself at a distance from the rest of the world. He was an island, remote and inaccessible. Billy Martin was one of the few ballplayers who had a knack for reaching him. In some incomprehensible manner, he had found a bridge to DiMaggio.

Yet to see Joe play baseball, even in his final years, was to see baseball as a form of art. It wasn't just natural talent. The "how" of how he did it seemed to be drawn from the same remote center that his outward persona expressed so well. It made him all the more fascinating.

He was instinctive as a center fielder. At the crack of the bat, he knew where the ball was headed. Many players make exciting grandstand plays because they're slow to respond to a ball hit their way. Joe didn't make circus catches. Instead, he glided like a clipper ship to the spot where the ball would descend. He stood and pounded his glove...and waited.

His swing was picture perfect, and when he was up at bat he read the pitcher as only a natural and intelligent hitter can do.

Putting aside his fielding talents, his batting average, and home run hitting ability, there was something else about him both indefinable and inspirational. He didn't have to say a word, but when he walked in the clubhouse, you felt his presence; when he took the field, you knew he was there. It was obvious that the other players responded to him. When he played, they played better, as if they were striving for perfection because perfection itself was on the field with them.

In 1951, Joe Di was just marking time. He was tired, worn out, and had confided to Pete Sheehy that he had had it – he would definitely retire at the end of the season. With time running out, I was always looking for an opening and I hoped that the train trip would provide the opportunity that had eluded me for more than two years.

I wondered all the time how to make the entree that would allow me to speak to him. I rehearsed some lines, none of which seemed particularly original or compelling. I even tagged along with Billy Martin. He didn't mind but it didn't seem to help.

Although I was at a loss, like a medieval knight in search of the holy grail, I wouldn't give up until I had attained my prize. I waited vigilantly for an opening to DiMaggio.

When our first game with Cleveland was over, the bus brought us back to the hotel lobby around six o'clock. I stuck with Phil, Billy, and Yogi, who were headed for the hotel restaurant in the lobby.

"Hey Joe, come here for a minute." I turned around. It was DiMaggio. I ran over, telling Rizzuto I'd catch up with him in a minute.

"Do me a favor."

"Anything you want, Joe," I answered.

"After you eat, get me a couple of magazines and bring them up to my room tonight because I feel like doing some reading." Joe handed me five dollars as he was speaking.

"Sure Joe," I said. "Anything in particular?"

"You know – Life, Look, the Sporting News, some local papers," Joe answered.

I couldn't believe this was happening. I couldn't have wished for a better opportunity.

"Joe, I'll get them right now if you want?"

"No. Go enjoy your dinner. I'm going to take a little rest anyway."

"Okay, Joe. I'll see you in about an hour."

When I rejoined Phil, Billy, and Yogi in the restaurant, the waitress was taking orders. The afternoon game with the Indians had made everyone hungry. Steaks again were the order of the day.

"So what did Joe want?" Billy asked me.

"Oh, nothing really," I answered, hoping that Billy would just drop the inquiry.

"Did he want you to get something for him?" Billy asked.

"Just some magazines," I answered reluctantly. "He told me

to bring them up after dinner."

"Never mind, Joe," said Billy. "I'll take care of it. Give me the money and I'll bring the magazines and papers to Joe myself. I want to see him anyway. He's like my best friend. I want to talk to him every chance I get 'cause I don't know if he's coming back next year."

In slow motion, I reached into my pocket and drew out the five-dollar bill. I couldn't even look at Billy because I was so mad and disappointed that there was no way I could control my expression. As I handed the five to Billy, Phil Rizzuto reached over and pushed my hand back to my pocket and turned to Billy.

"No Billy," Phil said. DiMaggio wants to be alone tonight. He's tired. Let young Joe get the magazines."

Billy looked like a child who had suffered the worst sort of rebuke. He sulked and turned angrily to his salad, attacking the lettuce with his knife and fork.

The dinner was brief and uncomfortable. Billy and Yogi left with Whitey Ford to catch a movie. Phil headed back to Room 1805 to relax in front of the television set. I went directly to the paper shop in the lobby and picked up the magazines and newspapers that Joe wanted.

It was about 7:30 when I knocked on the door to DiMaggio's room. He answered the door dressed in pajamas and a red silk bathrobe.

"Hi Joe," I said, as I put the magazines and newspapers on a dresser. "I think I got everything you wanted. If you need anything else let me know."

I headed slowly for the door but Joe motioned for me to sit down.

"What're you up to tonight?"

"I'll probably just go to the room and watch an old movie on the tv set."

"Well, there's no hurry. It's not even eight. Stay for awhile. I was just going to call room service for dinner. Why don't you join me?"

"Maybe I'll just have a Coke. I already ate dinner with the guys."

"By the time they bring my dinner up, you'll be hungry again. How about a ham and cheese sandwich?"

"Sure," I said, not wanting to take a second look at an opportunity like this.

"So, how do you like train travel?" Joe asked.

"I love it. It's really the first time I've ever been away from home. Kind of special."

"First time?"

"Yeah. That's why I'm rooming with Phil. It was the only way my mom would let me go."

"You and Phil are pretty close, aren't you?"

"He's like a big brother to me."

"That's good. Phil's a swell guy."

Just then the doorbell rang. Dinner had arrived.

I had heard that Joe was treated like royalty in all the cities we visited and he never waited long for service. It was rumored that the bell boys competed with one another for the honor of serving DiMaggio his dinner and that after he signed the check, the bell boys never turned in the tabs. They knew those mementos bearing Joe's signature would be collectors' items some day.

Joe was right. At age fifteen, it doesn't take long to build up an appetite. As I bit into my ham and swiss, Joe said, "I know you have been going around to the other players asking them what did it take for them to succeed in the major leagues. I remember you asked me that question one time."

I nodded. 'This is it! this is it!' I said to myself.

"That was a long-term assignment my grammar school principal gave me two years ago," I said between bites.

"It was a condition he set for allowing me to leave school early when the Yankees play at home."

"I always wondered if you were cutting classes," Joe said with a smile.

I laughed. "My parents wouldn't let me do that. I had to have Brother Colombo's permission. He told me I could do it if I kept my marks up and spent my time with the Yankees discovering the essential ingredients of a successful baseball player."

Joe added, "Perhaps it's more important to discover what makes a person successful."

"I really think that was Brother Colombo's idea."

As I sipped my Coke and he drank his coffee, Joe said, "Well, what have you learned so far?"

"My first lesson was about compassion. That came from Jackie Robinson. My first day on the job, I was the visiting bat-boy during an exhibition game with the Dodgers. I felt nervous, like a complete stranger in the visitor's clubhouse. My brother Ralph wasn't there to ease me through it. I guess Jackie saw me sitting alone. He seemed to know how I felt. He came over, put his arm around me, and bought me a Coke and said to put it on his bill."

"And what did you learn from that," Joe asked.

"It's important to be aware of other people's feelings – to

have a sense of what they're going through."

"And did you tell Brother Colombo about that experience?" Joe asked.

"I did. Brother Colombo told me that I had probably learned on the first day the most important lesson that life has to offer... that is, do unto others...."

I noticed that I had caught Joe's attention. I had finished the sandwich and Coke and said that it was probably time for me to go.

"Stay for a while. Those old movies will be on all night," Joe said.

"Tell me some of the other lessons you learned."

"Bobby Brown says you have to have a goal to succeed," I answered. "You have to know where you want to go and how to get there. Phil Rizzuto told me that he has to compensate by trying harder because of his size. And Yogi told me that there's two kinds of baseball players – the natural, who can just flick his wrists and knock the ball out of the stadium, and the good hitter, who uses ninety-nine percent perspiration and one percent inspiration. Yogi says you and Mickey Mantle are naturals."

"Who's a good player?" Joe asked.

"I guess you could say Billy Martin is a good player."

Joe smiled when I said that. Except for Casey Stengel, he probably knew Billy better than anyone.

"You know Joe," DiMaggio said, "I never thought about what makes a successful baseball player or a successful person. But you brought that question to me a while back, and I have been giving it some thought."

I was on the edge of my seat – as if everything I had hoped or worked for rode on what he would say to me. I wanted some part of the essence, the mystery of DiMaggio to be revealed in his words. For myself, I wanted to understand, because I longed to be like the players that I spent my young life with. I wanted to play with Rizzuto's enthusiasm. I wanted to imbibe Jackie Robinson's persistence. I wanted to be as motivated as Frank Shea and to concentrate my energies like Joe Page. They were great ballplayers. To me they were great people. But Joe DiMaggio – he was greatness itself. How could I ever be like him if I didn't understand what was inside him. I needed to hear it in his own words.

"Joe, I promise, I'll give you my answer by the end of the year."

"Okay, Joe," I said, trying with the greatest effort to mask my disappointment.

"Thanks for the sandwich and for this time. It meant a lot to me that we sat and talked like this."

"I enjoyed it too, Joe. Go and enjoy the movie. I'll see you tomorrow."

I left Joe's room and walked to the end of the hallway. I stared out the window at the Cleveland skyline and, beyond, at the vastness of Lake Erie.

"So close, so close," I whispered to myself. Would there be another day, another opportunity. Not like today. I was sure of that.

My last, best hope was that Joe would keep his promise. I held onto it with all I had inside me. I hoped that he would remember. I knew that I would never forget.

22

The next generation

A few days later, the team left Cleveland and headed to Detroit. I got into the rhythm of traveling by train, sleeping in hotels, and spending every waking moment with my new family. The night games provided the only difficult adjustment. When a night game was over, we wouldn't get back to the hotel until after midnight. By the time I had had a late night snack in the hotel restaurant and "chewed the rag" with the guys, it was one or two in the morning. After a couple of nights of this, it was starting to catch up to me.

During a night game in Cleveland, I had to fight to keep my eyes open. A couple of nights later in Tiger Stadium, I lost the fight. I was startled to hear Casey's voice, "Carrieri, grab a bat and pinch hit for DiMaggio."

I jumped up and ran for the bat rack. The dugout roared with laughter. I'm sure I was red in the face, but I guess I had it coming.

On the way to the Sunday afternoon game in Detroit, Frank Crosetti had the bus driver take a detour to one of the Catholic churches in town. It didn't seem to matter to Crosetti that half the players on the bus weren't Catholic. It was Sunday, so Crosetti figured we ought to go to church. Mom would've been happy to know.

Billy Martin, who never ceased to amaze, seemed right at home inside the church. He left Crosetti, Rizzuto, Berra, and me in the pew so that he could go to confession before Mass started. I stared in disbelief as he stood outside the confessional, rosary beads in hand, waiting to go inside the box.

After seven innings of the Sunday game, the Yankees were beating Detroit 1 to 0. Gil McDougald stepped into the batter's box to lead off the eighth inning. Gene Woodling was in the on-deck circle. I rubbed my eyes. I felt certain that McDougald and Woodling were batting out of turn. I had stacked the bats in the rack before the game as I always did. Woodling's bat was slotted first, McDougald's second. By game rules, if McDougald took one pitch, he was automatically out.

I didn't know what to do. What if I was wrong. I had no proof, just my memory of how I stacked the bats that day. Casey changed the lineup so often, I told myself, I might have gotten my days crossed. And if I stopped the game for nothing, I'd look like a fool and might not outlive the abuse I was bound to get. Casey had the scorecard in his back pocket, so there was no way to check without going to the source.

What I did next said more about Casey Stengel than it did about me. Casey was a master at making people perform for him. I think some of the younger ones – like his "son" Billy Martin – did it out of love for the old man. Other players did it simply to keep their jobs. Hank Bauer, who platooned in right field with Cliff Mapes, told me once that he was dying to take himself out of the second game of an endless doubleheader one hot, muggy summer afternoon.

"Joe, I was so exhausted, I thought I was going to collapse," Hank said. "But I wouldn't dare take myself out. If I did, who knows when Casey would put me back in the lineup."

I was keenly aware of Casey's presence. After all, he put in a word with my principal, Monsignor Waterson, that cleared a path for me from Cardinal Hayes High to Yankee Stadium for the afternoon games. And Casey recognized me as he showed so well after our first game in Cleveland. If there was a way I could repay Casey's kindness, I wouldn't hesitate.

That's why I couldn't sit still. I quickly pulled up alongside Casey, perched as he always was on the top step of the dugout scanning the playing field. He seemed a little annoyed at first, as if I had broken his concentration. I tried to tell him that McDougald was batting out of turn, but I was too excited and wasn't making a great deal of sense. Time was running out. McDougald had dug in at home plate and was just about ready to take the first pitch.

"Call time, Case," I yelled.

"Huh?"

Casey was a little hard of hearing and there was a lot of background noise. He cupped his hand to his ear.

"Call time," I hollered as loud as I could.

At the last possible second, he ran out of the dugout and yelled "Time." The home plate umpire threw his hands up and the game came to a halt.

"What's up Joe?"

If he was angry with me, it just wasn't coming through.

"Gil's batting out of turn. I'm sure of it."

Casey's face had a look of exaggerated shock. But this time, he wasn't mugging for the sportswriters. He was really upset. He fumbled for the scorecard in his back pocket. When he finally got it out and looked at it, he threw his hands up as if he had just gotten news of a death in the family. He looked toward home plate and shouted, "Mr. McDougald, can I see you for a moment?"

Noticing Casey with his scorecard, the home plate umpire took his out. The field umpires and the Tiger's manager converged at home plate, and pretty soon everyone was comparing notes.

In fact, McDougald was batting out of turn. Chagrined, McDougald exchanged places with Woodling, who also was looking none-too-happy. But I guess it helped Woodling's concentration. He got a single and eventually scored the winning run as the Yankees took it 2 to 1.

Casey rarely held press conferences on the road. But he called one that day in Detroit. As he explained to the sportswriters, "I didn't call you together to discuss a trade or the acquisition of a bonus baby. I want to answer for baseball fans the question that is on everybody's mind…that is, what makes the Yankees great.

"The Yankees are not great because of Joe DiMaggio or Mickey Mantle or Yogi Berra. They are not great because of any one individual. The Yankees are great because they play as a team. And any organization is as strong as its weakest link and the Yankees have no weak links. Every Yankee carries his own weight. Even our batboy."

Since many of the reporters were in the dark about the goings-on in the eighth inning, Casey explained how my sharp eyes saved the day for the Yankees. Casey then called me up in front of the assembly and presented me with a $25 check as a token of his appreciation for my alertness and, as he termed it, for being a contributing member of his family.

The next day, my mom and dad delighted to read in the New York Daily News, the Journal American, and the Herald Tribune how the batboy saved the day for the Yankees. I'm sure they didn't notice Casey's ruminations on Yankee greatness. It wouldn't have registered with Mickey and Yogi either. But I'm sure it stung Joe Di to hear that he was just another link in the chain, albeit a golden chain.

For years, Joe Di led the Yankees by example. Whether in his prime or in his final pain-filled years, Joe was the white knight whose very presence on the field of battle was enough to carry his team to victory. He offered little in the way of verbal encouragement. But Joe's leadership was charismatic, inspiring others to follow him while drawing on the best in themselves.

Casey, on the other hand, was an orchestrator. He managed the Yankees to greatness with a carrot and stick. He wanted the younger players to take their cues from him. And in his desire to build a dynasty, Casey perceived early on that the key to his success rested with Joe Di's heir apparent, Mickey Mantle.

Mickey was the dominant figure in the up-and-coming generation of Yankees; the powerful engine that could pull the Yankees to World Series championships for years to come. Great things were expected of him. He quickly impressed the baseball world with his bat, provoking comparisons to the greatest power hitter ever – Babe Ruth.

Although Mickey wasn't tall (listed officially by the Yankees as 5'11", he was probably an inch shorter), he had a weight lifter's neck, broad shoulders that tapered to a narrow waist, huge wrists, and forearms like Popeye. He was commonly described as a football coach's all-American dream-come-true. Where it counted most, however, he had the perfect baseball build, with the long loose muscles in his arms like DiMaggio and Williams. And when he first came to the Yankees, he was probably the fastest man in baseball.

But Mickey was painfully shy. While Joe Di's reserve kept people at a respectful distance, Mickey's awkwardness prompted others to try and draw him out. Phil Rizzuto extended himself to Mickey as he naturally did with the "youngsters" on the team. Casey, though, lavished attention on Mickey.

Billy Martin also formed a fast friendship with Mickey. In my quest to define the qualities of a successful baseball player, on the train between Chicago and St. Louis I asked Mickey about the ingredients that made him successful. He looked puzzled and at a loss for words, but Billy quickly answered for him.

"It's simple Joe. Mickey has strength and speed. Because Mickey is so strong and hits a ground ball or a one hopper so hard, the infield has to play back or someone's going to have a line drive whiz past his ear or a one hopper bounce off his shins. But because he's so fast, he can lay down a bunt and get a single nine times out of ten."

Billy was a catalyst for Mickey. He pumped up his confidence and ignited his enthusiasm. During the time on the train, Billy pressed Mickey time and again about bunting his way on base.

I often wondered what drew the two of them together. I think each supplied for the other some element missing in himself. Billy could get along with anyone and he helped Mickey adjust to the demands that came with being a celebrity – even going so far as to answer questions for Mickey. Billy liked Mickey because he was a star attraction. It was the same chemistry that drew Billy to Joe Di. As much as Billy desired attention, Billy at his best was someone "who could learn to hit good." He knew that his talents would never command the respect that DiMaggio's or Mantle's did. But if Billy couldn't be in center stage, he was always just to the left or right of it.

"If you bunted one time out of four, you'd be the batting champion," said Billy.

"I'm not comfortable with it," said Mickey. "I foul the ball or I just plain miss it."

"Hey Rizzuto," said Billy, "we got a job for you. You got to teach Mickey how to bunt."

"Okay. Just wait till I finish this hand."

Phil was playing cards a few tables away with Berra, Raschi, and Reynolds. He came over in a minute to hear what Billy was talking about.

"We think that with Mickey's speed, he could hit .400 if he learned how to bunt," said Billy.

"Let's find out," said Phil. "We can start tomorrow."

The next day in St. Louis, Phil instructed Mickey about how to hit the bunt.

"You have to practice it right," said Phil. "If you don't, you'll only get worse each time you try it."

Phil lectured Mickey for quite a while in the dugout on how to hold the bat, how to take it from his shoulder to his side in a fluid motion, and how to place the ball. But Mickey had little patience for Phil's lecturing. He wanted to get on the field for the hands-on instruction. "Not so fast," said Phil. "You've got a lot to learn."

Shortly, though, Billy stood on the pitcher's mound, I played along the third or first base line depending on the side of the plate Mickey was swinging from, and Phil provided the hands-on instruction. Because the Yankees were the visiting team though, barely enough time was allotted for batting and fielding practice let alone an extended bunting tutorial for Mickey. After a short stint, we stopped and Phil made him promise to wait until the team's return to Yankee Stadium before he tried to bunt his way on in a game.

On the road, the physical and emotional intensity of Mickey and the other young players like Billy, Whitey, and Hank Bauer, stood in sharp contrast to that of the team's veterans. Life on the road had a slow and leisurely pace that suited the older guys. They arrived in the hotel restaurant about nine or a little after and sat down to a hearty breakfast. Afterwards, there was time to shower, dress, have another cup of coffee and read the sports pages. The team bus left for the ballpark at about eleven and returned to the hotel by six or so. In the evening, the older players retired early. Joe Di needed a maximum amount of time to restore his energy for the next day's game. Phil liked to relax in front of the tv set. Others played cards. Although some of the family men like Vic Raschi missed their wives and kids on these extended road trips, the major wrinkle to this comfortable lifestyle was the night games.

"Every night game I play takes one day off my career," Johnny Mize often said. The practice of playing under the lights was only a few years old, but the older players in particular longed for the good old days when games were played exclusively by the light of day.

In contrast, Mantle, Martin, Bauer, and Ford were just hitting their stride when the older guys were ready to turn off the lights. They had enough energy, stamina, and interest to keep going all night and still be ready for the next day's game.

Once, in St. Louis, Billy and Mickey were out late at some local night spot, definitely having a drink or two, too many. Casey had an eleven o'clock curfew in effect, and both Casey and his detective were in the hotel lobby counting heads as the players walked through the lobby. Like a good parent, Casey didn't want to close his eyes until he knew that all his players were home in bed.

By two a.m., everyone was accounted for, except Mickey and Billy. Casey was concerned and sent his hired gun to check all the local hot spots for his wayward sons. When the detective reported back that the boys were nowhere to be found, Casey collared the house detective, and the trio took the elevator to the eighteenth floor. Casey had the house detective open Billy's door first. Much to everyone's surprise, Billy was in bed, sound asleep. When they walked down the hall to Mickey's room and opened his door, he, too, was in a deep sleep.

Next day, Billy laughingly told his story to Bauer, Berra, and Rizzuto. The duo sneaked in after curfew while Casey was dozing in the lobby. The boys didn't have their keys and they didn't want to ask at the front desk in case they'd be noticed in the lobby at that late hour. They went to the eighteenth floor and knocked on a door down the hall from their own rooms. The occupant was happy to accommodate the Yankee celebrities, and allowed them to climb out his window onto an eighteen-inch ledge. From there, they crawled to their respective rooms and went to sleep.

When you consider that they weren't operating with optimal coordination, they were taking a pretty big chance. Billy swore the listeners to secrecy and if Casey ever got the full story, he never let on. Casey exerted a lot of control, but as regards the younger players, his attitude was, "boys will be boys."

On the first game day back in New York, Mickey, Phil, Billy and I arrived early at Yankee Stadium to continue with Mickey's bunting education. Before our eyes, Mickey developed from a proficient bunter into a very dangerous one.

As the season wore on, Mickey did bunt more often and, if it was possible, he became a more talented and dangerous hitter than he already was. To the delight of New York fans, he even bunted his way on base in the 1951 World Series.

Mickey wasn't meant to be a bunter though. Great warriors, like Mickey, fight their battles with big clubs. People came to the ballpark to see him murder the ball. He didn't let them down. The Yankees won their third straight pennant in 1951, finishing ahead of the Cleveland Indians by five games. Although, they had now won three straight pennants, DiMaggio's departure seemed imminent and it was obvious that an era's end was fast approaching.

Somehow, decade after decade, the Yankee tradition was recreated, and, on the broad shoulders and big bats of players like Ruth, Gehrig, and DiMaggio, it was carried into the next generation.

Although in 1951 the Yankees had an abundance of talent, youthful energy, and team spirit, it was doubtful that their winning ways would continue. There was no player with DiMaggio's stature and experience to whom the torch could be passed.

Into this void stepped the true successor to the tradition of Yankee greatness – Casey Stengel. In the pantheon of Yankee heroes, he will be remembered as they are – not so much for their heroic exploits or personal achievements – but for his contribution to an enduring baseball tradition and for upholding

the measure of baseball greatness to which others would jealously aspire.

23

The promise

The 1951 season ended on a triumphant note for the Yankees. World Champions once again, they beat the New York Giants in six games. Joe Di hit a home run, two doubles, and drove in five runs during the subway Series that extended the Yankees' dominance of major league baseball for the third straight year.

Although most people believed that Joe would call it quits, he kept us guessing. The Series showed he still had some of his old magic and he didn't make any announcement after Game 6 at Yankee Stadium on October 10th. Since that would have been the perfect time to let the world know that he was retiring, I held out some hope that he might return.

Joe DiMaggio had been a young player of great promise. He kept that promise to his fans. During the thirteen years that he played with the Yankees, his team won ten pennants and nine World Series. He had a lifetime batting average of .325 and belted 361 home runs. His numbers would have been even better had he not lost three prime years to military service during World War II. Although his contemporary, Ted Williams, played longer and compiled more impressive statistics, the City of Boston still waits for the "Curse of the Babe" to pass. The Red Sox have not won a World Series since 1918, the second-to-last year Babe played for Boston before he was traded to the

Yankees. DiMaggio never played only for himself. His personal successes carried his team to victory year after year.

When the Series was over, I never really got to bid him farewell and good luck. There were always so many people around the clubhouse – his teammates, the press, celebrities – he seemed more removed from me than ever. Although he never answered my question, I held out some hope that he'd be back in 1952.

If he didn't return and I never got to talk to him again, I told myself, "that's part of life." Some things you just have to accept. With all the things that DiMaggio had to think about, how was he going to remember a promise he made to me in the middle of the summer in Cleveland. Who was I anyway? Just the batboy. He had much more important things to consider – like how he was going to spend the rest of his life.

By November, my focus had started to shift to my sophomore year studies and the upcoming basketball season at Cardinal Hayes High. I had a five-month respite from the Yankees, although I was bound to check in with Pete Sheehy from time to time. I also read the sports pages regularly. Although the coverage focused on college and professional football, I didn't want to miss a story about DiMaggio's retirement, should it occur.

About a month after the end of the World Series, I got a phone call from Sheehy. It was Saturday, he was at the Stadium (of course), and was he excited.

"Joe, you've gotta come over here right away. DiMaggio stopped by to pick up some things and he said he'd like to see you."

"He wants to see me?" I asked.

"I just said that, didn't I," Pete answered.

I couldn't believe what I was hearing. Joe Di wanted to talk to me. I had hardly answered, "Sure, I'll be right over" before I grabbed my coat and hat ran out of the house.

I didn't have the patience to wait for the Concourse Bus. Instead, I ran the twenty-eight blocks from my house to Yankee Stadium in a matter of minutes. Out of breath, I banged on the clubhouse door. Joe Serrano let me in.

DiMaggio was sitting at one of the big picnic tables in the center of the clubhouse with Pete. Joe was drinking coffee, Pete a beer.

"It didn't take you long," Pete said.

"I came as fast as I could," I answered.

"I'm sorry I didn't get to say good-bye to you, Joe," I said. "I'm still hoping that I'll see you next year."

"That's part of the reason I'm here," he answered. "You won't be seeing me in the clubhouse next year, Joe. This is it for me and I wanted to say good-bye."

"Gee, Joe, I'm really sorry to hear that…everyone will be sorry to hear that," I said, my voice filling with emotion.

"I guess you know why I asked you to come here?"

"Not really," I said (not meaning a word of it).

"You know Joe, I told you that I'd think about your question. I told you that a while back and I try to keep my promises. And I have given it a lot of thought."

"You have?" I said, barely able to contain my pleasure at the honor that Joe Di was bestowing on me.

"Joe," he continued "the last couple years have been tough. I knew I wouldn't be playing much longer and I really thought of hanging it up after the '49 season. But I decided to come back at least for 1950. I'm glad I did.

"Because I was a little older, a little more tired, I had forgotten the fun and enthusiasm that I had once found in the game of baseball. But in 1950, I met Billy Martin, and Billy helped me to rediscover something I had forgotten along the way.

"Billy loves baseball. He loves to talk about baseball and he wants to be the best. And although I couldn't play the game the way I did when I was Billy's age, because of Billy I remembered...the excitement...the fun...and I learned to appreciate all the things I had experienced.

"You're probably wondering what all this has to do with the meaning of success, Joe. Well, it's this.... Remember to stay interested in the game. You're always a student. And as long as you live, you always have more to learn. If you can remember that, you'll have learned a great deal about the meaning of success."

There were tears in my eyes as I struggled to thank him. I don't know if I was more choked up by Joe's words or by the fact that he had kept his promise to me, the Yankee batboy. But I've never forgotten – either his kindness or the last words he spoke to me that November day.

Joe Di made it official in December 1951. At a press conference he announced that he could no longer produce for Yankee fans the kind of baseball that their loyalty deserved. It seemed as if things would never be the same.

24

The real thing

Over the years I spent with the Yankees I developed a strong relationship with Phil Rizzuto. I always looked up to him and when my own brother left the team before the 1952 season, I felt closer to Phil than ever. At age sixteen, to me, Phil was the real thing, and if someone asked me who I'd want to be when I grew up, I wouldn't have hesitated to say that I'd like to be Phil Rizzuto.

Phil came of age when Italian-Americans were coming into their own and beginning to distinguish themselves in many areas. This was particularly true of Yankee players of that era, which, in addition to Rizzuto, included such great Italian surnames as DiMaggio, Berra, Raschi, and coach Frank Crosetti – not to mention the most colorful Italian of all – Billy Martin. It meant a lot to me, son of an Italian immigrant, to have a friend like Phil. For me, Phil was the Italian connection – someone to be proud of, someone to look up to.

In 1952, he asked me to help him answer the considerable amount of fan mail that he received at Yankee Stadium. Since Phil had given me a typewriter when I started high school, I told him I'd be happy to do it. I handled the correspondence on the weekends and Phil paid me $20 a week for this job.

You get to know someone very well by the type of letters he receives from his fans and friends. Phil was always doing favors for people, whether it was getting them free tickets to baseball games, or recommending someone for a job. I caught the flavor of Phil early on, and didn't have any trouble incorporating the "real Phil" into the letters that I wrote for him.

Phil received religious items of all kinds, including rosary beads and medals dedicated to a variety of saints. Rings, bracelets, and other items of jewelry were commonly included with the letters. Fans solicited his donations to a variety of worthy causes and some more questionable ones – "Phil, could you loan a dedicated fan of yours $...?"

A good many letters came from fans who didn't simply ask for an autographed picture. Instead, they asked for advice on how to become a major league player, how to play shortstop, what foods to eat, what programs he recommended to strengthen their muscles. With letters like these, I'd sit down for a couple of minutes each week and go over the answers with Phil; then I'd type a short response to the fan, signing Phil's name.

Phil knew about my agreement with Brother Colombo from the beginning. Coming from a background similar to mine, he wanted to know more about my principal. Sitting on a bus as we motored around Cleveland in 1951, I told him Brother Colombo was an Irishman, about 35 years old, with a round, angelic face, prematurely bald, a ready smile and a happy disposition.

"Now I know what he looks like, but what's his philosophy – how does he think?" Phil asked. "By the assignment he gave you, he sounds like a very unusual person."

I took a minute to think about that one. I had known Brother Colombo for most of my young life, so the answer wasn't far away.

"He thinks God gave us all talents, and that we have to discover those talents, and use them as best we can," I said. "No matter how big or small our talent may be, God will show us how to put it to good use."

Over the years, I had heard Brother Colombo say that more times than I could remember.

"I couldn't agree with him more," said Phil. "God has a grand design for everyone and gave each of us sufficient ability to succeed. The trick is to find out what you are good at and then give it your all, pay the price, and keep working at it."

"Tell me, Joe," Phil said, "if I turn the tables and asked Brother Colombo what his definition of success is, what do you think he'd say?"

"I don't really know," I answered. "He never really told me. I think he wanted me to find that answer for myself. But from knowing him, I think he feels success is measured not by how many friends you have and how popular you are, but how much good you do for other people."

I looked at Phil and said, "You know, Brother Colombo could have been talking about you."

The Yankees of the early 1950s were a hot property. World Champions again and again, everyone wanted a piece of them. Requests came in all the time for players to appear on radio and television programs as guests or contestants. These opportunities even filtered down to the Yankee batboy and ballboy.

Since I was a little older and wearing a Yankee uniform, the Yankee management felt comfortable sending me to represent the team. Often I got these opportunities because the players hated to do these public relations spots and would go to great lengths to avoid them. As a low man on the roster, these assignments naturally came my way.

At first, I was reluctant to go – mostly because I was a typical adolescent, self-conscious about my looks, how I dressed, how I sounded. In time, I got over my shyness and learned to be myself in front of a camera or a microphone.

Phil frequently asked me to stand in for him when he couldn't (or didn't want to) appear on a television or radio program. This happened during the 1952 season when George Weiss, the Yankees' General Manager, wanted Phil to appear on a popular television program.

"Phil," he said, "I want you to appear on Jack Parr's quiz show – Bank on the Stars."

"When is it George?" Phil asked.

"Next Saturday."

"Gee, I'd love to go" – (I knew he didn't mean it) – "but the team will be in Cleveland that night, George."

"That's right" Mr. Weiss said, "I had forgotten."

Phil then put his arm around my shoulder. "You know George, if you want someone to represent the Yankees, Joe'll do a fine job."

Mr. Weiss turned to me and asked, "Do you want to go on television with Jack Parr?"

I started to shake my head, all the while trying to think up a good excuse. As I began to shake my head though, it quickly flashed through my mind that I'd be letting Phil down if I said "no."

"Sure, I'll do it, Mr. Weiss," I said.

"Okay, Joe. We'll let them know our batboy is coming."

Saturday night came quickly. Mom, Dad, Ralph, and I took the cab to the television studios on 53rd Street in Manhattan. I was quickly ushered in to see Mr. Parr. As he was being made up, he ran through some of the questions he would be asking me that evening. He told me that before the game began he would be asking me a little bit about myself, my school, and my experiences as the Yankee batboy. He also told me that I would have a partner on the show, a beautiful blond perfume sales-woman.

"I'm going to ask her what she wears," said Mr. Parr, "and she's going to answer, 'Chanel No. 5.'"

"Then, I'm going to turn to you, introduce you as a sixteen-year-old boy from the Bronx, and ask you what you wear. Okay, Joe?"

"That's fine with me," I said.

"Then, you're going to say 'I wear nuttin.'"

I didn't respond. Here I was on television, with my whole family in the audience, being asked to do something I felt really uncomfortable with. The whole conversation with Jack Parr would make me look like a knucklehead from the South Bronx who couldn't respond to a question in a complete sentence.

Soon I was under the lights with Jack Parr and my beauti-ful blond partner. When the program started at 8 p.m., Jack Parr asked her, and then me, some questions about ourselves. He then turned to her and said, according to plan, "You smell lovely tonight. What are you wearing?"

"Mr. Parr, I wear Chanel No. 5 perfume."

"That's lovely."

He turned to me and said, "And Joe, what are you wear-ing?"

He was all smiles, waiting for me to deliver the punch line that would give the audience a good laugh.

"Mr. Parr, I'm wearing cologne."

No one in the audience laughed. Jack Parr gave me a killing look and had all he could do to keep the corners of his mouth up. But there was something in my background that wouldn't let me play along. And there was my pride as a Yankee. A Yankee would never allow himself to be a fool of, and certainly wouldn't make a fool of himself.

After watching a short film clip, my partner and I were asked some questions about what we had seen. We gave the three correct answers: three bags of gold; a cardinal; and José Ferrer.

To my family's delight, I went home with $152.50.

A week later, when the Yankees were back in town, I told Phil how I refused to go along with making a fool of myself. As the product of a working class, Italian family, from a New York City neighborhood, Phil understood instinctively why I wouldn't tell Jack Parr that "I wear nuttin."

He patted me on the back and said, "You made the Yankees proud."

25

The tryout

In the South Bronx where I grew up, baseball was everything. Kids then weren't interested in basketball or football; few families had televisions and kids had time to spare. It wasn't unusual for my friends and me to hike to the baseball fields on Randall's Island where, on a Saturday or Sunday, we'd play baseball for eight hours or more. Big hits, great catches, and baseball statistics fired our imaginations and inspired our play.

We talked about nothing else. Everyone I knew was either a Yankees or Giants fan and the battle lines were drawn over philosophical questions like: "Who's the greatest living long ball hitter, Mantle or Mays?" That argument ran for years. We read the sports pages religiously and we actually felt close to the ballplayers. Of course, I was in the Yankees' locker room all season long. But for my friends, it was only a short hop from our neighborhood to Yankee Stadium and only a few blocks further to the Polo Grounds. New York was a safe place then, and our parents felt comfortable letting us go to watch a game or a practice provided we were in the company of a "responsible" adult – usually someone's older brother.

Before I actually worked there, Yankee Stadium inspired a cathedral-like sense of awe and wonder in me. When I first stepped on the field as a thirteen-year old batboy, though, I was star-struck. I embraced it all – from the sweet smell of the infield grass to the granite monuments in center field dedicated to Yankee heroes of bygone days. If ever there was a place to spend the rest of my life, this was it.

Everyone I knew dreamed of being a ballplayer when he grew up. Most of them knew that their chance of playing was as remote as the stars in the Bronx sky. I thought I had a better shot. I was a good pitcher in grammar school and had developed into a solid outfielder and an even better hitter at Cardinal Hayes High. And I was running the inside track because I knew everyone connected with the Yankees. I never doubted that I would be a hard-throwing, home run hitting, great fielding, pinstripe-wearing Bronx Bomber. As I climbed the clubhouse ladder, first as visiting batboy, then ballboy, then batboy for the World Champion Yankees, I grew in anticipation of the day that I could make this dream come true.

For three years, I had seen other dreamers come and go. A few times each summer, the Yankees sponsored tryouts for the local talent. Although the team was on the road whenever the Yankees held this event, I came in to help Pete Sheehy guide the Yankee hopefuls in, around, and out the clubhouse.

Toward the end of the 1952 season, when I was almost seventeen, I told Pete that I finally wanted to take my shot. "Why not," Pete answered. "You know how it works. Fill out an application and send it to Paul."

I was hoping for a little more encouragement from the master of the clubhouse, but Pete was the essence of understatement. I took his advice, though, filled out my application and sent it to Paul Krichell, the head scout at Yankee Stadium. I also convinced several of my friends to take a shot at greatness with me.

Bobby Corbo, Junior Rosenberg, and Bobby Seidel said "why not" when I asked them to join me. They weren't really serious about playing for the Yankees, but their day at Yankee Stadium would earn them bragging rights for a lifetime.

I joined about 150 other aspiring ballplayers who would've sacrificed life and limb to play ball with the World Champion Yankees. We tried out, fifty at a time, over a three day period. Thirty players – the ten best from each group – would be brought back the following Saturday to play an exhibition game under the watchful eyes of Paul Krichell and his scouts.

I laughed inside when I witnessed the child-like excitement of the guys as they changed their clothes in Mickey's, Whitey's, and Yogi's locker. If I didn't spend half the days of the year in the clubhouse, I would've felt the same sense of pride they showed as they walked through the corridors, locker room, and runways of the house that Ruth built.

When we had dressed and assembled around the picnic tables in the clubhouse, Mr. Krichell opened with a monologue that I knew by heart. But this time it was different. This one counted and I hung on every word.

"You boys are here to show us that you can play in the major leagues. Baseball is a great sport that builds bodies and character. But not everyone is cut out to be a major leaguer. And let me tell you that natural talent isn't everything you'll need to play for the Yankees. There's something even more important. It's a thing called character. Because if you're a great player but not a great person, you don't belong here. Character is a tradition on the New York Yankees. Troublemakers don't belong on this team. And if, by some mistake, the wrong man makes the cut, he's not going to stay here very long."

The place was breathlessly still when, finally, he hollered "All right, let's go. Come on and show us what you've got."

We burst from the clubhouse into the bright light of a summer afternoon. Soon, everyone had a number pinned on the back of his shirt that would be his identity for the rest of the day. Paul and his two assistants divided the group into three and each headed off to a different part of the field with the Yankee hopefuls in tow. My Yankee scout, clipboard in hand, wrote down our numbers and began to do the drills that measured throwing, running, fielding, hitting, base running, strength, agility and some intangible called "head motivation and desire."

After we did a few laps around the running track to loosen up, the scout began the first drill – a sixty yard wind sprint – that pitted one boy against another. After everyone had his turn, we were tested on our infielding ability. The scout hit fungoes to see how well we covered the infield and to find out if we could make the long, accurate throw to first and the quick flip to second to start a double-play. Next, we were roaming the outfield, living off memories of Joe DiMaggio as we pulled in the long drives that were hit our way. Each time a boy finished a drill, the scout made a check or note on his clipboard. The pitchers were spared most of this, and went to the sidelines where a different scout tested them for speed and control.

I knew I was making a good showing. It didn't hurt that I had played the infield at Yankee Stadium for hundreds of practices or that I knew just what it took to make a precise throw from deep center to second base. But in spite of that, I was a Yankee – I was good and I wasn't afraid to show what I had. I knew my speed, fielding ability, and throwing arm had impressed my scout. I was in a good position to make the first cut.

The last test was hitting against my old friend "Iron Mike." Many a morning, I had dragged this pitching contraption – aptly named by the Yankee players – out of the bullpen to the pitching mound so Billy Martin or Hank Bauer could sharpen his batting skills. After a few adjustments, Iron Mike shot the balls at 85 to 90 mph with superb accuracy. As a reward for shagging the balls and reloading the pitching machine, I frequently got my turn at Iron Mike after practice was over.

Most of the young men had never hit against a pitching machine, and based on the surprised look on many faces, a lot of them had never even seen one. This was an enormous advantage for me. I hit just about everything thrown my way. My best shot ended up in the left center field seats. My scout looked impressed.

At the end of the session, all fifty of us regrouped in the clubhouse where Paul Krichell read out the numbers that were invited back the following Saturday. I had made it. My friends, none of whom made the cut, were excited for me and promised to come back the next Saturday to cheer me on.

In a few days, I was back at the Stadium, where the thirty survivors divided into teams of fifteen. This time, we weren't hitting against Iron Mike, but against an array of young pitchers determined to show their stuff. They had speed, but little control. I managed to get a single in three times at bat – not bad, considering the poor pitches I had to swing at. Although I made a good showing overall, the competition seemed better this time. I didn't walk into the clubhouse with the same confidence I possessed a few days earlier.

Mr. Krichell and the other scouts followed us into the clubhouse after the game was over.

"Six young men have what we think it takes to begin a career with the New York Yankees," Krichell began. "I have contracts here for each one of them. If your number is called, please stay behind to see me. For the rest of you men, I want to thank you for trying out with the New York Yankees. You're good ballplayers and each one of you has potential. Don't be discouraged. If you didn't make it this time, come back and see us again next year. All right, listen up."

"My number's got to come up," I whispered to myself. "It's got to." I stopped breathing as Paul Krichell read one number, then a second, a third.... But my number was never called.

I could barely talk when I met Junior Rosenberg, Bobby Corbo and the others outside the Stadium gate. They had watched the whole game.

"Who got the contracts?" Bobby Corbo asked.

"Three, Six, Eight, Fourteen, Seventeen, Twenty-one, Twenty-seven," I muttered.

"Number Eight got a contract. And Fourteen got one too," said Bobby Corbo. "Are you kidding me? That can't be right, Joe. You were a whole lot better than Number Eight and Fourteen never even hit the ball. Don't take it lying down. If those guys got contracts, you should've gotten one too."

"Definitely. Go back and talk to Mr. Krichell," Junior said.

"Go back and get your contract, Joe. You deserve it," said the rest of my friends.

I had never been a sore loser and, if it were another time or something less important, I would have walked away. But this was different. I ran back into the clubhouse and nearly knocked over Pete Sheehy.

"What's the rush, Joe," Sheehy asked. "I thought the tryout

was over."

"It is for me," Pete. "I didn't make it and I want to know why. I was at least as good if not better than two of the guys who made the cut."

"Go straighten it out with Paul," was his answer. "Tell him what's on your mind. He's in the umpire's room."

I was filled with false courage when I knocked on the door to the umpire's room. I banged even harder when no one answered right away.

"Who is it?" came the voice from inside.

"Joe the batboy."

"Come on in."

"What can I do for you?" Mr. Krichell said as I walked through the doorway. "You know, you did pretty good today."

"Well, that's the reason I'm here, Mr. Krichell. My friends watched the game today and they thought I should've gotten a contract."

"That's fine Joe. You want a contract, you've got it."

"You're kidding," I said.

"Absolutely not. You go to Alabama in two weeks. We'll pay you $150 a month to play on our farm team down there and we'll see what happens."

My heart sank and I was dizzy. "Alabama" I said to myself. "I'll have to quit high school…leave my parents."

I must've looked stunned because Mr. Krichell immediately said, "If you want the contract, let me know in a week because the other boys are going to Alabama the week after next and we'll need a little time to make the arrangements."

"Okay. I'll just go home and talk it over with my parents. I'll get back to you by next week."

"You know where to find me, Joe."

I ran into Sheehy on the way out. "What happened?" he asked.

When I explained Mr. Krichell's offer, Sheehy said, "If you go Joe, we're going to miss you." And then it hit me like a screaming subway. If I signed the contract, there was no more Yankee batboy, no more Yankee Stadium, no more Phil, Billy, Mickey, or Whitey. But how could I turn down a chance to be a New York Yankee.

When I rejoined my friends outside the Stadium, they were thrilled for me. So was my brother Ralph when I told him the news at home. "Joe, this is your opportunity. If this is what you really want, then go after it."

Ralph's words struck a nerve. Now I had to make a decision and I wasn't so sure that this was what I really wanted. When I told Mom and Dad, they acted as if they were happy for me, but I could tell that, deep down, they didn't really want me to go. I knew they'd miss me and I knew they'd worry.

"What is it you really want Joe," Mom asked.

"I'm not sure. I'm happy with everything here, but this is the chance of a lifetime and I'm afraid I might blow it if I don't go."

"Why don't you go talk with Brother Colombo," Mom said. "He's always been interested in you. He'll know what's best. Go talk to him."

I had been out of St. Jerome's Grammar School for more than two years, but I was never a stranger to my old principal. He was never more than a few blocks away. I often visited him at my old school on 136th Street between Alexander and Willis Avenues. I had also been over to the brothers' residence on

Alexander Avenue about a block from the school, which is where I headed the day after my tryout with the Yankees.

Brother Colombo lived in a two-story brownstone with the other brothers who taught at St. Jerome's. An invitation or appointment wasn't required and Brother Colombo always seemed to enjoy visits from his old pupils. When I arrived, Brother Colombo and Brother Anthony were sitting on the front stoop. No one in my old neighborhood had air-conditioning, and community life in the summertime centered around the front steps of our buildings where we escaped from hot-box apartments to the evening cool.

"How's it going Joe? Out for a walk?"

"It's going good. But I have something I want to talk over with you, Brother Colombo."

My tone must've been abrupt because Brother Anthony quickly picked up and said, "Oh. Okay. I think I'll go upstairs and do some reading."

As soon as Brother Anthony was inside the door, I said, "Brother, I got a problem."

"Big problem, Joe?"

"Big enough, Brother. I had a tryout with the Yankees yesterday. I did well, but I didn't make the final cut. But I went back to the head scout, Mr. Krichell, and told him that I thought I was as good as some of the guys who made it."

"And what did Mr. Krichell have to say?"

"He threw me a curve. He told me that if I wanted a contract, it was mine for the asking. I have to leave in two weeks for Alabama. They'll pay me $150 a month to play for their farm team down there."

"Big decision. What're you going to do?"

"That's the million dollar question, Brother. I mean, I'd be giving up a lot – high school, my family, my job as batboy. But I always dreamed of playing for the Yankees. I mean...it's my dream and I think if I don't grab it, it may not come my way again."

"So why are you hesitating?"

"Because I was always so sure that this was what I wanted. But now that it's real...."

"You're having some doubts," Brother Colombo finished my sentence.

"I guess you could say that."

"Why do you want to be a Yankee, Joe?"

"Who wouldn't want to be a New York Yankee?"

"You're not answering my question. Why do YOU want to be a Yankee?"

"The best times of my life have been with the New York Yankees. I don't want to imagine that it's ever going to end."

"Describe for me one of those best moments."

"I can think of plenty, Brother. I can think of Joe DiMaggio at bat in the bottom of the ninth with men on base and the Yanks down by a couple of runs. The house is full and everyone is on the edge of his seat. It's a smoldering fire, ready to explode if Joe Di can just provide the spark. He knocks the ball out of the park and burns the house to the ground. It's so noisy, you can't hear yourself think. The dugout empties and surrounds Joe Di as he crosses home plate. He's carried the day. If that's not the best feeling in the whole world, I don't know what is."

"Everyone wants to be a hero, Joe. But tell me something... I asked you three years ago to find out what makes a successful ballplayer. What have you learned from the Yankees?"

"I've learned that you need persistence, talent, goals, motivation. You can't succeed without them.

"Was there any one answer that meant more to you than the others...or something that was especially important to you, Joe?"

"Well...maybe there were two. Phil Rizzuto's always said something similar to you...something like God has a plan for all of us. We should try and find out what it is, and then work at it with everything we've got."

"You know I like that answer."

"I knew you would."

"Anything else?"

"Just something Joe DiMaggio said to me...something about staying interested because you always have so much more to learn."

"I like that answer as well, Joe. Look, you've learned so much from the Yankees. You're getting to the point where you have to internalize what you've learned. Wearing pinstripes may or may not be in God's grand design for you, and no matter what you do, you'll always have more to learn. Just give it some time, Joe."

"I don't want to miss an opportunity."

"This isn't the only opportunity life has to offer you. You're intelligent. You're a good student. Use what God gave you. You have chances that your mother and father couldn't have dreamed for themselves. Use your head. Finish high school. Go to college. If you still want to play baseball, great. It'll be there for you. If it's meant to be, you'll know it. But don't pass up all these other opportunities. Your chance at an education is the one thing that may never really come your way again."

"Okay Brother," I answered with a note of resignation.

"Listen, sleep on it Joe. You'll know what to do. By the way, what do you think of Willie Mays?" said the die-hard Giants fan. "Best hitter I've seen in years."

"He's good, Brother. But he's no Mickey Mantle. Mickey's the best home runner hitter since Babe Ruth."

"No. I don't think so. I was in the Polo Grounds the other week when Willie hit one out...."

I never did play for the New York Yankees. But I helped a classy outfielder who needed some help through the application process. Arturo Lopez regularly showed up at ballfields around the South Bronx where my friends and I played at night or on the weekend. He knew I was the batboy for the Yankees and had been offered a contract after my tryout. I got an application for him, filled it out, and sent it in to Yankee Stadium. Mr. Krichell and company must've been pretty impressed. A few years later, I watched him play the outfield in Yankee Stadium.

Not long after my tryout with the Yankees, during the 1952 World Series with the Dodgers, Charlie DiGiovanna said, "Joe. I heard about your tryout. Why not come and play for us. Seriously. The Dodgers are having tryouts later this month."

"No thanks. Maybe in a couple of years," I said.

"Give it a try Joe. What do you have to lose. I'll even buy you lunch."

"Well...seeing as you're buying, I'll give it a try."

A couple of weeks later, after the Yankees had again won the World Series against the Dodgers, I took the very long subway ride from my Bronx neighborhood to Ebbets Field in

Brooklyn where I joined thirty or forty Dodger hopefuls. Charlie introduced me to the head scout and told him that the Yankees had offered me a minor league contract.

"That so," he said. He seemed interested. I wasn't though, and treated my Brooklyn tryout as a lark.

Charlie advised me that the scouts liked outfielders with a strong arm from center field. "Throw it as hard as you can," Charlie said. Not wanting to disappoint him, I made a point of throwing the ball over the catcher's head whenever I fired the ball in from center field.

After the tryout, I didn't stick around the clubhouse to see if my number was called. Charlie and I slipped out to the manager's office where Charlie delivered on his promise – two ham and cheese sandwiches. When I was about to leave, Charlie walked me out the clubhouse through the underground passageways and back to the subway that would deliver me from Dodgerland.

"Take care Joe. We'll be seeing you next year."

"Maybe so. If the Giants don't get there first."

"The Giants. Never happen."

I started to walk downstairs to the subway when Charlie hollered, "Hey Joe."

"Yeah," I said, as I turned around.

"About the tryout...."

"What about it?" I said.

"Don't give up your day job," he answered with the biggest, broadest grin I had ever seen him wear.

26

Synchronicity

There are perfect moments in life. I remember a late summer evening at Yankee Stadium...toward the end of a long double-header. The sun was sinking behind the right field seats. It was cooling a bit. The infield was shaded, and as I stood by myself at the end of the dugout, the grass filled my head with the mellow ripeness of late summer. I sipped a Coke, that had never tasted, nor ever would, taste so sweet. The crowd had thinned and quieted. Everyone was bone-tired. But not a tiredness born of exhaustion. Instead, the muscles were so heavy and achy that they seemed to disappear and leave behind a sense of elation – the self-satisfaction of having done a thing well – of completing something important, like crossing the finish line of a long race.

1955 was my last year with the New York Yankees. I had graduated Cardinal Hayes High and was now in my sophomore year at Fordham University in the Bronx. I suppose Brother Colombo knew me better than I knew myself. By this time, I was immersed in my studies and had my eyes set on law school a few years down the road.

By the time I left the Yankees, the team had started flying in and out of American League cities. Gone were the long, leisurely, pleasure-filled hours in the train's club car. Instead of a thirty-four hour train ride, the team flew non-stop from Kansas

City to New York in about four hours time. It was thrilling to pick out Yankee Stadium through the clouds as the airplane descended toward LaGuardia Airport.

There was at least one holdout, though. Frank Crosetti, Mr. down-to-earth, wasn't the least bit interested in soaring above the clouds. In fact, he was petrified. He rode the rails back to the Big Apple as he always had as player and coach.

But everything changes. I guess Frank took a lot of ribbing about his earth-bound ways. The next year when I returned to the dugout for a visit, Frank made a point of identifying for me the different aircraft winging their way above Yankee Stadium on their way to LaGuardia or Idlewild. Whether through love or necessity, Frank overcame his fear of flying and became an aficionado of air travel.

When I started out with the New York Yankees as a thirteen-year-old, I could hardly get across a busy street without my big brother's help. What I learned during my seven seasons with the Yankees was how to overcome my fears, to make my own decisions, and to believe in myself. Ralph, Brother Colombo, my parents, and the Yankees saw me through those years when a child becomes a man. And I can say without qualification that I owe them a debt of gratitude that I can never fully repay.

Since imitation is the sincerest form of flattery, it was only natural that I should want to play for the New York Yankees. But if I learned anything during my seven years with the team, it was that each person has to find his own talents, to work at them, and then, at some point, to trumpet them for his own satisfaction and to share them for the benefit of others.

I remember a year in the early 1950s when Bill Dickey, the Yankees' batting coach, tried to get Hank Bauer, the Yankee outfielder, to refine his short choppy swing into a smooth powerful one. Bauer, an ex-Marine, was an enormously powerful guy who consistently hit about .280. Not bad, but Dickey was certain that Bauer could hit .325 if he learned to swing at the ball like Joe DiMaggio. Bauer reluctantly took his coach's advice and soon fell into a deep slump.

"Just give it a little more time," Dickey said. "Be patient."

But the slump continued and, in a matter of weeks, Bauer was hitting far off his usual pace. After another poor performance at the plate, he finally confronted Dickey and said, "Look, I'm Hank Bauer, not Joe DiMaggio." The next at bat, he was again swinging that short, choppy swing, and, pretty soon, he was hitting like the Hank Bauer of old.

I was never meant to hit the ball over the center field fence or steal second base before sixty thousand cheering fans. But as Bauer told Dickey, or as Rizzuto or Brother Colombo told me many times, I had an obligation to find out for myself what my gifts and talents were and I had to learn to be myself.

There was a synchronicity to the Yankee teams of the early 1950s…a fortuitousness of circumstances and events that brought together the right mix of talent, leadership, and inspiration to create teams of unsurpassed quality. For the Yankees, it seemed as if all things worked together for their good. I've often had the same feeling about my life – a conspiracy of positives that helped me grow and develop as a person.

I had such an opportunity with some of the greatest baseball players of all time. Although I never took the field with the New York Yankees, their legacy lives on in my life and in the lives of my children. For hardly a day goes that I don't say to at least one of the six of them (or to one of my four grandchildren):

"set goals for yourself;" "be persistent;" "practice;" "focus;" "find your talents;" "be yourself;" "find out where you fit in God's grand design;" or "Did I ever tell you about the time that Joe DiMaggio said to me? ..."

Despite the groans and the sounds of "O Dad" or "There he goes again," I know they listen.

You can never repay a gift. But you can learn to give yourself. I hope that in remembering and appreciating the Yankees, Brother Colombo, and my family, I can affirm what they did for me and I can pass on to my children lessons that have lasted a lifetime and that, for me, a former Yankee batboy from the South Bronx of New York City, have made all the difference.

27

Epilogue

How do you close the circle? How do you finish the race? How do you bring it home?

In writing *Searching for Heroes* I've tried to remember and share what baseball meant to me as I grew from a child into a young man. Baseball wasn't a pastime, it was how I grew up. It provided for me – a boy who lived in a closely-knit, narrowly focused world – a vital connection to a world beyond. It carried me to cities I could only dream about and gave me experiences that opened my eyes to the future. Baseball also gave me a connection to the people I shared my life with as well as to millions of others whom I never met. America's passion for baseball was universal.

More than anything else, though, the game of baseball was about the players themselves. They were larger than life. They understood intuitively that they were heroes and knew that people, particularly kids, were always watching them. Perhaps one great difference between then and now is that most of them felt an obligation to live up to those expectations. In the late '40s and early '50s, with memories of Babe Ruth's enormous love for children freshly in mind, a player would never knowingly let a kid down.

Some people may question whether I really could have

cared so deeply for what players might have told me about how to succeed, about how to live life. But that's really why kids went to the ballpark in the first place. Ballplayers showed you, a base at a time, what you had to do next and how to find your way home. Great ballplayers showed you how to live life greatly. The answers that ballplayers gave to my incessant questioning were a confirmation of what I saw on the playing field. Games were won by players who demonstrated great persistence, who loved what they were doing and never lost interest in it, who maximized their talents to reach their goals.

In some ways, I ended far away from the playing fields of the Bronx. I graduated college, went on to law school, and began practicing law. Instead of playing center field for the Yankees, I developed an active adoption practice in New York.

For me, though, adoption law is a confirmation of all the values I learned with the Yankees. It is a way of connecting children with their own heroes – parents who will love them, give them a home, and a sense of value and importance. What we tried to do for Terrence of Zimbabwe in chapter one of this book is similar to what the Yankees did for me. They nurtured and protected me until I was ready to be on my own. They gave me a chance so that I could make my own life. That's something I am still doing in my law practice and that I will continue to do for the rest of my life. It's my way of saying with gratitude – I will never forget.